STILL STEAMING

The Guide to Britain's Steam Railways 2002-2003

EDITOR
John Robinson

Sixth Edition

British Library Cataloguing in Publication Data
A catalogue record for this book is available from the British Library

ISBN 1-86223-058-7

Copyright © 2002, MARKSMAN PUBLICATIONS. (01472 696226)
72 St. Peter's Avenue, Cleethorpes, N.E. Lincolnshire, DN35 8HU, England

Printed by Bookcraft.

ACKNOWLEDGMENTS

We regret that we have been unable to include captions for the photographs which are included in this publication due to lack of space. Many were taken by our own photographer but we do thank the railways which so generously provided the remaining photographs.

We aim to improve the quality of photographs in future editions and welcome any which readers may wish to supply.

The cover photograph of the Appleby Frodingham Railway Preservation Society's Peckett tank engine was taken in November 2001 when it was on loan to the Elsecar Steam Railway. It has since been returned to The Corus Steelworks at Scunthorpe.

FOREWORD

Following the continued success of Still Steaming in 2001 we have added a number of new locations for this revised 6th edition.

We were greatly impressed by the friendly and cooperative manner of the staff and helpers of the railways which we selected to appear in this book, and wish to thank them all for the help they have given.

Although we believe that the information contained in this guide is accurate at the time of going to press, we, and the Railways and Museums itemised, are unable to accept liability for any loss, damage, distress or injury suffered as a result of any inaccuracies. Furthermore, we and the Railways are unable to guarantee operating and opening times which may always be subject to cancellation without notice.

If you feel we should include other locations or information in future editions, please let us know so that we may give them consideration. We would like to thank you for buying this guide and wish you 'Happy Steaming'.

John Robinson

EDITOR

Note: Further copies of this guide may be obtained, post free, from our address shown on page 2 of this book.

CONTENTS

DAY OUT WITH THOMAS UK EVENTS 2002

MARCH

29th March – 1st April	Embsay & Bolton Abbey Railway
29th March – 7th April	Mid Hants Railway
23rd – 24th March	Steam – Museum of the Great Western Railway
29th March – 1st April	East Anglian Railway Museum
29th March – 1st April	Gwili Railway
30th March – 1st April	Cholsey & Wallingford Railway

APRIL

4th – 7th April	Dean Forest Railway
5th – 7th April	North Norfolk Railway
13th – 14th April	Middleton Railway
20th – 21st April	Middleton Railway
20th – 21st April	Spa Valley Railway
27th – 28th April	Spa Valley Railway
27th – 28th April	Gloucester Warwickshire Railway
27th – 28th April	Mangapps Railway Museum

MAY

4th – 6th May	South Tynedale Railway (Friends of Thomas Event)
4th – 6th May	South Devon Railway
4th – 6th May	Mangapps Railway Museum
4th – 6th May	East Lancashire Railway
4th – 6th May	East Somerset Railway
4th – 6th May	Northampton & Lamport Railway
4th – 6th May	Chinnor & Princes Risborough Railway
	(3rd May open only to Lord Taverners disabled outing)
4th – 6th May	Pontypool & Blaenavon Railway
5th – 6th May	Fairbourne & Barmouth Railway (Friends of Thomas)
11th – 12th May	Avon Valley Railway
11th – 12th May	Shackerstone Railway
11th – 12th May	Severn Valley Railway
18th – 19th May	Severn Valley Railway
18th – 19th May	Swindon & Cricklade Railway
18th – 19th May	Shackerstone Railway
18th – 20th May	Bo'ness & Kinneil Railway
25th – 27th May	Great Central Railway
25th – 26th May	Bure Valley Railway

JUNE

1st – 4th June	Embsay & Bolton Abbey Railway
1st – 2nd June	Paignton & Dartmouth Railway
1st – 9th June	Eastleigh Lakeside Railway
1st – 5th June	Dean Forest Railway
1st – 4th June	Foxfield Steam Railway
1st – 4th June	Vale of Glamorgan Railway
1st – 9th June	Midland Railway Centre
4th – 5th June	Fairbourne & Barmouth Railway (Friends of Thomas)
8th – 9th June	Colne Valley Railway
10th – 14th June	Colne Valley Railway (Learn With Thomas Event)
15th – 16th June	Colne Valley Railway
17th – 21st June	Colne Valley Railway (Learn With Thomas Event)
14th – 16th June	Buckinghamshire Railway Centre
15th – 16th June	Nottingham Transport Heritage Centre
15th – 16th June	Sittingbourne & Kemsley Light Railway (Friends of Thomas)
15th – 16th June	Bluebell Railway
15th – 16th June	North Yorkshire Moors Railway
18th – 23rd June	Gwili Railway
15th – 27th June	Kent & East Sussex Railway (includes Learn With Thomas)
22nd – 23rd June	Bluebell Railway
23rd June	Romney, Hythe & Dymchurch Railway (Friends of Thomas)
22nd – 23rd June	Colne Valley Railway
22nd – 23rd June	Kirklees Railway
22nd – 23rd June	Nottingham Transport Heritage Centre
29th – 30th June	West Somerset Railway
29th – 30th June	Welshpool & Llanfair Light Railway

JULY

6th – 7th July	Welshpool & Llanfair Light Railway
6th – 7th July	Mangapps Railway Museum
6th – 7th July	Elsecar Steam Heritage Centre
6th – 7th July	Shackerstone Railway
13th – 14th July	Buckinghamshire Railway Centre
13th – 14th July	Shackerstone Railway
13th – 14th July	Mangapps Farm
20th – 21st July	Eastbourne Miniature Railway
20th – 24th July	Churnet Valley Railway
20th – 21st July	Crich National Tramway Museum
20th – 21st July	Darlington Railway Museum

JULY (continued)

20th – 21st July	Isle of Man Steam Railway
27th – 28th July	Crich National Tramway Museum
21st July	Romney, Hythe & Dymchurch Railway (Friends of Thomas)
26th July – 4th August	Bodmin & Wenford Railway
26th – 29th July	Isle of Wight Steam Railway
28th – 29th July	Fairbourne & Barmouth Railway (Friends of Thomas)
27th – 28th July	Kirklees Railway

AUGUST

3rd – 4th August	Llangollen Railway
3rd – 4th August	Chinnor & Princes Risborough Railway
10th – 11th August	Gloucestershire Warwickshire Railway
3rd – 11th August	Midland Railway Centre
3rd – 4th August	South Downs Light Railway
7th August	South Downs Light Railway
9th – 11th August	Bo'ness & Kinneil Railway
8th – 12th August	Cleethorpes Coast Light Railway (Friends of Thomas)
10th – 17th August	Mid Hants Railway
10th – 11th August	Middleton Railway
9th – 11th August	East Lancashire Railway
10th – 11th August	South Downs Light Railway
17th – 26th August	Great Central Railway
17th – 18th August	East Somerset Railway
16th – 19th August	Bressingham Steam Museum
17th – 25th August	Strathspey Steam Railway
18th – 19th August	Fairbourne & Barmouth Railway (Friends of Thomas)
17th – 18th August	Foxfield Steam Railway
24th – 26th August	Northampton & Lamport Railway
23rd – 26th August	Pontypool & Blaenavon Railway
23rd – 26th August	East Anglian Railway Museum
24th – 26th August	Embsay & Bolton Abbey Steam Railway
29th August – 1st September	Dean Forest Railway
31st August – 1st September	Severn Valley Railway

SEPTEMBER

7th – 8th September	Eastleigh Lakeside Railway
7th September	Romney, Hythe & Dymchurch Railway (Friends of Thomas)
6th – 8th September	Buckinghamshire Railway Centre
7th – 8th September	Severn Valley Railway
7th – 8th September	North Yorkshire Moors Railway

7th – 8th September	Swindon & Cricklade Railway
14th – 15th September	Sittingbourne & Kemsley Light Railway (Friends of Thomas)
21st – 22nd September	Keighley & Worth Valley Railway
21st – 22nd September	Kent & East Sussex Railway
28th – 29th September	Kent & East Sussex Railway
28th – 29th September	Colne Valley Railway
28th – 29th September	Bure Valley Railway

OCTOBER

4th – 6th October	Didcot Railway Centre
5th – 6th October	Colne Valley Railway
5th – 6th October	Ravenglass & Eskdale Railway (Friends of Thomas)
5th – 6th October	Avon Valley Railway
5th – 6th October	East Lancashire Railway
5th – 6th October	Shackerstone Railway
19th – 27th October	Llangollen Railway
19th – 20th October	Elsecar Steam Railway
19th – 20th October	Mangapps Steam Museum
19th – 21st October	North Norfolk Railway
19th – 22nd October	Midland Railway Centre
26th – 27th October	Steam – Museum of the Great Western Railway
19th – 20th October	South Tynedale Railway (Friends of Thomas)
26th – 27th October	Great Central Railway
26th October – 3rd November	Swanage Railway
26th – 27th October	Mangapps Railway Museum

NOVEMBER

9th – 10th November	Middleton Railway
9th – 10th November	Northampton & Lamport
16th – 17th November	Middleton Railway

DECEMBER

7th – 8th December	Buckinghamshire Railway
7th – 8th December	Telford Steam Railway
7th – 8th December	Barrow Hill Roundhouse
13th – 15th December	Telford Steam Railway
13th – 15th December	Didcot Railway Centre
14th – 15th December	Barrow Hill Roundhouse
21st – 22nd December	Barrow Hill Roundhouse
21st – 22nd December	Telford Steam Railway
21st – 22nd December	Didcot Railway Centre
26th December – 5th January	Eastleigh Lakeside Railway

THE FRIENDS OF THE NATIONAL RAILWAY MUSEUM

This organisation was formed in 1977 to help conserve and operate railway exhibits that might otherwise have to wait many years before returning to public view. The organisation is run on a membership basis which imparts a number of privileges which include:

- free admission to the museum whenever it is open to the public.
- the *NRM Review*, published quarterly, which keeps Friends in touch with events at the Museum, carries information about the National Collection locomotives, features articles of general railway interest and includes authorative reviews of videos and books.
- opportunities to work as a volunteer in the Museum.
- invitations to FNRM members meetings in York and London.

MEMBERSHIP DETAILS – Normal membership is valid for 12 months from date of registration.

Category	Rate
Ordinary	£18.00
Unwaged	£13.50
Junior (Under 18)	£9.00
Family	£27.00
Retired Couple	£20.25
Group	£30.00
Life (below 60)	£ 270.00
Life (60 and over)	£200.00
Life (retired couple)	£300.00
Life (family)	£400.00

Apply for membership to:

FNRM
National Railway Museum
Leeman Road
York
YO26 4XJ

Family Membership – is for a maximum of four persons, two or three of whom are under 18 years of age, residing at the same address

Retired Couple Membership – is for two persons aged 60 or over and not in employment.

Covenanted Membership – if you are a taxpayer, your subscription can be covenanted to produce extra revenue for the Friends. Please ask for more details from the Friends Office.

Charities Aid Foundation – we can accept subscriptions by CAF cheque or CAF charity card.

NATIONAL RAILWAY MUSEUM

Address: National Railway Museum, Leeman Road, York YO26 4XJ
Telephone Nº: (01904) 621261
Year Formed: 1975
Location of Line: York
Length of Line: Short demonstration line

Nº of Steam Locos: 79
Nº of Other Locos: 37
Nº of Members: Approximately 3,500
Annual Membership Fee: £18.00
Approx Nº of Visitors P.A.: 500,000
Web site: www.nrm.org.uk

GENERAL INFORMATION

Nearest Railtrack Station: York (¼ mile)
Nearest Bus Station: York (¼ mile)
Car Parking: On site long stay car park
Coach Parking: On site – free to pre-booked groups
Souvenir Shop(s): Yes
Food & Drinks: Yes

SPECIAL INFORMATION

The Museum is the largest of its kind in the world, housing the Nation's collection of locomotives, carriages, uniforms, posters and an extensive photographic archive. Special events and exhibitions run throughout the year. The Museum is the home of the Mallard – the fastest steam locomotive in the world and Shinkansen, the only Bullet train outside of Japan.

OPERATING INFORMATION

Opening Times: Open daily 10.00am to 6.00pm (closed on 24th, 25th and 26th of December)
Steam Working: School holidays – please phone to confirm details
Prices: Free admission for all (excludes 'Friends of Thomas' events)
Phone (01904) 686263 for further details.

Detailed Directions by Car:
The Museum is located in the centre of York, just behind the Railway Station. It is clearly signposted from all approaches to York.

ALFORD VALLEY RAILWAY

Address: Alford Station, Main Street,
Alford, Aberdeenshire AB33 8HH
Telephone Nº: (01975) 562811
Year Formed: 1980
Location of Line: Alford – Haughton Park
Length of Line: 1 mile

Nº of Steam Locos: 1
Nº of Other Locos: 3
Nº of Members: Approximately 70
Annual Membership Fee: £15.00
Approx Nº of Visitors P.A.: 19,500
Gauge: 2 feet

GENERAL INFORMATION

Nearest Railtrack Station: Insch (10 miles)
Nearest Bus Station: Alford (200 yards)
Car Parking: Available on site
Coach Parking: Available on site
Souvenir Shop(s): Yes
Food & Drinks: No

SPECIAL INFORMATION

The Grampian Transport Museum is adjacent to the
Railway.

OPERATING INFORMATION

Opening Times: Weekends in April, May and
September. Open daily in June, July and August.
Trains run from 1.00pm to 4.30pm
Steam Working: The first Sunday of May, June, July
and August only.
Prices: Adult Return £2.00
      Child Return £1.00

Detailed Directions by Car:
From All Parts: Alford is situated 25 miles west of Aberdeen on the Highland tourist route. Take the A944 to reach
Alford.

APPLEBY FRODINGHAM RAILWAY

Address: Appleby Frodingham Railway Preservation Society, P.O. Box 44, Brigg, North Lincolnshire   DN20 8DW
Telephone Nº: (01652) 656661
Year Formed: 1990
Location of Line: Corus Steelworks, Scunthorpe

Length of Line: 18 miles of track
Nº of Steam Locos: 3
Nº of Other Locos: 2
Nº of Members: 60
Annual Membership Fee: –
Gauge: Standard
Web site: www.afrps.co.uk

GENERAL INFORMATION
Nearest Railtrack Station: Scunthorpe (2 miles)
Nearest Bus Station: Scunthorpe (2 miles)
Car Parking: Large free car park at the site
Coach Parking: At the site
Souvenir Shop(s): None
Food & Drinks: None

SPECIAL INFORMATION
A selection of Rail tours and Brake Van tours are operated over a distance of 7 to 18 miles of the steelworks internal railway system.

OPERATING INFORMATION
Opening Times: Selected weekends throughout the year which must be pre-booked via (01652) 657053 or e-mail – bookings@afrps.co.uk
Steam Working: See above
Prices: Free of charge
Please note that children cannot be carried on Brake van tours due to the open verandahs.

Detailed Directions by Car:
Exit the M180 at Junction 3 onto the M181, at the end turn right onto the A18. Take the 3rd exit at the roundabout (still on the A18) and turn left onto Ashby Road at the next roundabout. At the following roundabout turn right into Rowland Road and at the end of the road turn right then left into Entrance E. Car parking is available on the left and the path to the station is on the right.

AVON VALLEY RAILWAY

Address: Bitton Station, Bath Road, Bitton, Bristol BS30 6HD	**N° of Steam Locos**: 6
Telephone N°: (0117) 932-7296	**N° of Other Locos**: 3
Year Formed: 1973	**N° of Members**: Approximately 500
Location of Line: Midway between Bristol and Bath on A431	**Annual Membership Fee**: £13.00
	Approx N° of Visitors P.A.: 80,000
	Gauge: Standard
Length of Line: 2½ miles	**Web site**: www.avonvalleyrailway.co.uk

GENERAL INFORMATION

Nearest Railtrack Station: Keynsham (1½ miles)
Nearest Bus Station: Bristol or Bath (7 miles)
Car Parking: Available at Bitton Station
Coach Parking: Available at Bitton Station
Souvenir Shop(s): Yes
Food & Drinks: Yes

SPECIAL INFORMATION

The line is currently being extended through the scenic Avon Valley towards Bath.

OPERATING INFORMATION

Opening Times: Every Sunday from 5th May to 6th October + December weekends. Also Bank Holiday Mondays, Wednesdays in August and Christmas. Open from 10.30am to 6.00pm
Steam Working: 11.00am to 5.00pm
Prices: Adult £3.50
Child £2.00
Family Tickets £10.00
Senior Citizens £2.50

Detailed Directions by Car:
From All Parts: Exit the M4 at Junction 18. Follow the A46 towards Bath and at the junction with the A420 turn right towards Bristol. At Bridge Yate turn left onto the A4175 and continue until you reach the A431. Turn right and Bitton Station is 100 yards on the right.

BALA LAKE RAILWAY

Address: Bala Lake Railway, Llanuwchllyn, Gwynedd, LL23 7DD	**Nº of Steam Locos**: 3
Telephone Nº: (01678) 540666	**Nº of Other Locos**: –
Year Formed: 1972	**Nº of Members**: –
Location of Line: Llanuwchllyn to Bala	**Annual Membership Fee**: –
Length of Line: 4½ miles	**Approx Nº of Visitors P.A.**: 20,000
	Gauge: 1 foot 11 five-eighth inches

GENERAL INFORMATION

Nearest Railtrack Station: Wrexham (40 miles)
Nearest Bus Station: Wrexham (40 miles)
Car Parking: Adequate parking in Llanuwchllyn
Coach Parking: At Llanuwchllyn or in Bala Town Centre
Souvenir Shop(s): Yes
Food & Drinks: Yes – unlicensed!

SPECIAL INFORMATION

Bala Lake Railway is a narrow-gauge railway which follows 4½ miles of the former Ruabon to Barmouth G.W.R. line.

OPERATING INFORMATION

Opening Times: 29th March to 29th September
Steam Working: All advertised services are steam hauled. Trains run from 11.15am to 4.00pm.
Prices: Adult Single £4.00; Return £6.70
Child Single £2.00; Return £3.00
Senior Citizen Return £6.20
Family Tickets (Return): £8.00 (1 Adult + 1 Child); £16.00 (2 Adults + 1 Child). Additional Children are £1.50 each. Under 5's travel free of charge.

Detailed Directions by Car:
From All Parts: The railway is situated off the A494 Bala to Dolgellau road which is accessible from the national motorways via the A5 or A55.

BARROW HILL ROUNDHOUSE

Address: Barrow Hill Roundhouse, Campbell Drive, Barrow Hill, Chesterfield S43 2PR	**N⁰ of Steam Locos**: 4
	N⁰ of Other Locos: Over 40
	N⁰ of Members: 366
Telephone N⁰: (01246) 472450	**Annual Membership Fee**: £13.00 Adult
Year Formed: 1998	**Approx N⁰ of Visitors P.A.**: 10,000
Location: Staveley, near Chesterfield	**Gauge**: Standard
Length of Line: ¾ mile	**Web site**: www.barrowhill.org.uk

GENERAL INFORMATION

Nearest Railtrack Station: Chesterfield (3½ miles)
Nearest Bus Station: Chesterfield (3 miles)
Car Parking: Space available for 40 cars
Coach Parking: Available
Souvenir Shop(s): Yes
Food & Drinks: Yes – buffet

SPECIAL INFORMATION

The former Midland Railway roundhouse now provides storage and repair facilities for standard gauge locomotives and diesels.

OPERATING INFORMATION

Opening Times: Open daily throughout the year from 9.00am to 5.00pm
Steam Working: Special open days only – 13th, 14th, 20th & 21st July; 5th & 6th October; 7th, 8th, 14th, 15th, 21st & 22nd December.
Prices: Adult £7.00
Child £4.00
Family £17.00 (2 adults + 2 children)
Senior Citizen £4.00
Note: Driver training courses are available – please phone for further details.

Detailed Directions by Car:
Exit the M1 at Junction 30 and take the A619 to Staveley (about 3½ miles). Pass through Staveley, turn right at Troughbrook onto 'Works Road'. Continue along for ¾ mile, pass under the railway bridge and take the turn immediately on the right. Turn left onto Campbell Drive and the Roundhouse is behind Acorn Van Hire.

THE BATTLEFIELD LINE

Address: The Battlefield Line, Shackerstone Station, Shackerstone, Warwickshire   CV13 6NW
Telephone Nº: (01827) 880754
Year Formed: 1968
Location of Line: North West of Market Bosworth
Length of Line: 5 miles

Nº of Steam Locos: 7
Nº of Other Locos: 16
Nº of Members: 600 approximately
Annual Membership Fee: £11.00 Adult; £17.50 Family
Approx Nº of Visitors P.A.: 20,000
Gauge: Standard

GENERAL INFORMATION

Nearest Railtrack Station: Nuneaton (9 miles)
Nearest Bus Station: Nuneaton & Hinckley (9 miles)
Car Parking: Ample free parking available
Coach Parking: Can cater for coach parties
Souvenir Shop(s): Yes
Food & Drinks: Yes – Station Buffet

SPECIAL INFORMATION

Adjoining the Ashby Canal set in South Leicestershire's beautiful countryside, the Southern Terminus Station Shenton sits at the foot of the Battle of Bosworth Site (1485).

OPERATING INFORMATION

Operating Info: 2nd April to the last week in October. Please telephone for further details
Opening Times: 10.30am to 6.00pm
Steam Working: 12.30pm, 1.45pm, 3.00pm & 4.15pm on Saturdays & Sundays. Also from 11.15am during high season and Sundays.
Prices: Adult Return £6.00
　　　　　　Child Return £3.00
　　　　　　O.A.P. Return £4.00
　　　　　　Family Ticket £16.00
　　　　　　(2 adults and 2 children)

Detailed Directions by Car:
Follow the brown tourist signs from the A444 or A447 heading towards the market town of Market Bosworth. Continue towards the villages of Congerstone & Shackerstone and finally to Shackerstone Station. Access is only available via the Old Trackbed.

BEAMISH – THE NORTH OF ENGLAND OPEN AIR MUSEUM

Address: Beamish North of England Open Air Museum, Co. Durham   DH9 0RG
Telephone N°: (0191) 370-4000
Year Formed: 1970
Length of Line: ½ mile

N° of Steam Locos: 8
N° of Other Locos: 4
Approx N° of Visitors P.A.: 365,000
Web site: www.beamish.org.uk

GENERAL INFORMATION

Nearest Railtrack Station: Newcastle Central (8 miles); Durham City (12 miles)
Nearest Bus Station: Durham (12 miles), Newcastle (8 miles)
Car Parking: Free parking for 2,000 cars
Coach Parking: Free parking for 40 coaches
Souvenir Shop(s): Yes
Food & Drinks: Yes – self service tea room & licensed period Public House. Coffee shop in Summer.

SPECIAL INFORMATION

The Steam Elephant, a magnificent, full-size working replica of an early 'lost' locomotive from the 1800's (pictured left), makes its debut in Spring 2002. This amazing locomotive will be in action, alongside a replica of Locomotion N° 1, taking visitors on a short ride along the Museum's 1825 Railway.

OPERATING INFORMATION

Opening Times: Open all year round from 10.00am to 4.00pm in the Winter – open until 5.00 during the Summer. Closed Mondays and Fridays in the Winter.
N.B. There is a reduced operation in the Winter.
Steam Working: Daily during the Summer
Prices:
Adult £12.00 in Summer; £4.00 in Winter
Child £6.00 in Summer; £4.00 in Winter
O.A.P. £9.00 in Summer; £4.00 in Winter
Children under 5 are admitted free

Detailed Directions by Car:
From North & South: Follow the A1(M) to Junction 63 (Chester-le-street) and then take A693 for 4 miles towards Stanley; From North-West: Take the A68 south to Castleside near Consett and follow the signs on the A692 and A693 via Stanley.

THE BLUEBELL RAILWAY

Address: The Bluebell Railway, Sheffield Park Station, Nr. Uckfield, East Sussex, TN22 3QL
Telephone Nº: (01825) 720800
Information Line: (01825) 722370
Year Formed: 1959
Location of Line: Nr. Uckfield, E. Sussex
Length of Line: 9 miles

Nº of Steam Locos: Over 30 with up to 3 in operation on any given day
Nº of Other Locos: –
Nº of Members: 8,000
Annual Membership Fee: £15.00 Adult
Approx Nº of Visitors P.A.: 175,000
Gauge: Standard

GENERAL INFORMATION

Nearest Railtrack Station: East Grinstead (2 miles) with a bus connection
Nearest Bus Station: East Grinstead
Car Parking: Parking at Sheffield Park and Horsted Keynes Stations.
Coach Parking: Sheffield Park is best
Souvenir Shop(s): Yes
Food & Drinks: Yes – buffets and licensed bars & restaurant

SPECIAL INFORMATION

The Railway runs 'Golden Arrow' dining trains on Saturday evenings and Sunday lunchtimes. There is also a museum and model railway at Sheffield Park Station.

OPERATING INFORMATION

Opening Times: Open every weekend and also daily from May to September inclusive. Also open during School holidays and Santa Specials during December. Open from approximately 10.30am to 5.30pm
Steam Working: As above
Prices: Adult Return £8.00
            Child Return £4.00
            Family Return £21.50 (2 adult + 3 child)
            Senior Citizen Return £6.40

Detailed Directions by Car:
Sheffield Park Station is situated on the A275 Wych Cross to Lewes road. Horsted Keynes Station is signposted from the B2028 Lingfield to Haywards Heath road.

BODMIN & WENFORD RAILWAY

Address: Bodmin General Station, Losthwithiel Road, Bodmin, Cornwall PL31 1AQ	**Length of Line:** 6½ miles
Telephone Nº: (01208) 73666	**Nº of Steam Locos:** 10
Year Formed: 1984	**Nº of Other Locos:** 9
Location of Line: Bodmin Parkway Station to Bodmin General and Boscarne.	**Nº of Members:** 850

Address: Bodmin General Station, Losthwithiel Road, Bodmin, Cornwall PL31 1AQ
Telephone Nº: (01208) 73666
Year Formed: 1984
Location of Line: Bodmin Parkway Station to Bodmin General and Boscarne.

Length of Line: 6½ miles
Nº of Steam Locos: 10
Nº of Other Locos: 9
Nº of Members: 850
Annual Membership Fee: £9.00
Approx Nº of Visitors P.A.: 44,000
Gauge: Standard

GENERAL INFORMATION

Nearest Railtrack Station: Bodmin Parkway
Nearest Bus Station: Bodmin (¼ mile)
Car Parking: Free parking at site
Coach Parking: Free parking at site
Souvenir Shop(s): Yes
Food & Drinks: Yes

SPECIAL INFORMATION

The Railway has steep gradients and there are two different branches to choose from Bodmin General. Through tickets to "Bodmin & Wenford Railway" are available from all Railtrack stations.
Web site: www.bodminandwenfordrailway.co.uk

OPERATING INFO

Opening Times: Daily from 26th May to the end of September. Also daily during Easter – 24th March to 7th April. Open selected dates from March to May and also for Santa Specials in December. Approximately 10.00am to 5.00pm but also during the evenings in the Summer.
Steam Working: Usually trains are steam-hauled except for most Saturdays when Diesels are used.
Prices: Adult Return £5.00 to £8.00
Child Return £3.00 to £4.50
Family Return £14.50 to £22.00
(2 adults + up to 4 children)

Detailed Directions by Car:
From the A30/A38 follow the signs to Bodmin Town Centre then follow the brown tourist signs to the Steam Railway on the B3268 Losthwithiel Road.

BO'NESS & KINNEIL RAILWAY

Address: Bo'ness Station, Union Street,
Bo'ness, West Lothian   EH51 9AQ
Telephone Nº: (01506) 822298
Year Opened: 1981
Location of Line: Bo'ness to Birkhill
Length of Line: 3½ miles

Nº of Steam Locos: 21
Nº of Other Locos: 18
Nº of Members: 1,300
Annual Membership Fee: £14.00
Approx Nº of Visitors P.A.: 60,000
Gauge: Standard

GENERAL INFORMATION

Nearest Railtrack Station: Linlithgow (3 miles)
Nearest Bus Station: Bo'ness (½ mile)
Car Parking: Free parking at Bo'ness and Birkhill
Stations
Coach Parking: Free parking at Bo'ness Station
Souvenir Shop(s): Yes
Food & Drinks: Yes

SPECIAL INFORMATION

The Scottish Railway Exhibition is situated at Bo'ness
and conducted tours are also available of the caverns
of Birkhill Mine.

OPERATING INFORMATION

Opening Times: Open on weekends from April to
October. Also open Tuesday to Sunday in July and
August.
Steam Working: The first train leaves at 11.00am
and is steam-hauled as are all trains during the day.
The last train leaves at 4.15pm and is diesel-hauled.
Prices: Adult Return £4.50   Child Return £2.00
             Family Return £11.00
N.B. Group discounts are also available – please
phone for further details. Also, special fares and
timetables apply for special events.

Detailed Directions by Car:
From Edinburgh: Take the M9 and exit at Junction 3. Then take the A904 to Bo'ness; From Glasgow: Take the
M80 to M876 and then M9 (South). Exit at Junction 5 and take A904 to Bo'ness; From the North: Take M9
(South), exit at Junction 5, then take A904 to Bo'ness; From Fife: Leave the A90 after the Forth Bridge, then take
A904 to Bo'ness.

BOWES RAILWAY

Address: Bowes Railway, Springwell Village, Gateshead, Tyne & Wear NE9 7QJ	**Nº of Steam Locos**: 2
Telephone Nº: (0191) 416-1847	**Nº of Other Locos**: 4
Year Formed: 1976	**Nº of Members**: Approximately 70
Location of Line: Springwell Village	**Annual Membership Fee**: £12.00
Length of Line: 1¼ miles	**Approx Nº of Visitors P.A.**: 3,000
	Gauge: Standard

GENERAL INFORMATION

Nearest Railtrack Station: Newcastle Central (3 miles)
Nearest Bus Station: Gateshead Interchange (2 miles)
Car Parking: Free parking at site
Coach Parking: Free parking at site
Souvenir Shop(s): Yes
Food & Drinks: Yes

SPECIAL INFORMATION

Designed by George Stephenson and opened in 1826, the Railway is a scheduled Ancient Monument which operates unique preserved standard gauge rope-hauled inclines and steam hauled passenger trains.

OPERATING INFORMATION

Opening Times: During 2002: 1st & 21st April; 6th & 19th May; 3rd, 16th & 30th June; 7th & 21st July; 4th, 18th & 26th August. Also pre-booked only Santa Specials on 7th, 8th, 14th & 15th December.
Steam Working: Every 30 minutes
Prices: Adult Return £2.00
        Child Return £1.00
        Senior Citizens £1.00
(Prices include a train ride and a demonstration of the Rope Haulage inclines)

Web site: www.bowesrailway.co.uk

Detailed Directions by Car:
From A1 (Northbound): Follow the A194(M) to the Tyne Tunnel and turn left at the sign for Springwell; From A1 (Southbound): Take the turn off left for the B1288 to Springwell and Wrekenton.

BRECON MOUNTAIN RAILWAY

Address: Pant Station, Dowlais,
Merthyr Tydfil   CF48 2UP
Telephone Nº: (01685) 722988
Year Formed: 1980
Location of Line: North of Merthyr
Tydfil – 1 mile from the A465
Gauge: 1 foot 11¾ inches

Length of Line: 3½ miles
Nº of Steam Locos: 8
Nº of Other Locos: 1
Nº of Members: –
Annual Membership Fee: –
Approx Nº of Visitors P.A.: 70,000
Web site: www.breconmountainrailway.co.uk

GENERAL INFORMATION

Nearest Railtrack Station: Merthyr Tydfil (3 miles)
Nearest Bus Station: Merthyr Tydfil (3 miles)
Car Parking: Available at Pant Station
Coach Parking: Available at Pant Station
Souvenir Shop(s): Yes
Food & Drinks: Yes – including licensed restaurant

SPECIAL INFORMATION

It is possible to take a break before the return
journey at Pontsticill to have a picnic, take a forest
walk or visit the lakeside snackbar.

OPERATING INFORMATION

Opening Times: Daily from 29th March to 27th
October. Closed some Mondays & Fridays in April,
May, September and October.
Steam Working: 11.00am to 4.00pm
Prices: Adult Return £6.80
             Child Return (15 and under) £3.40
             Senior Citizen Return £6.20
             Dogs or Bicycles £1.00
             Family Rate – The first two children can
travel for £2.20 each when accompanied by an adult.

Detailed Directions by Car:
Exit the M4 at Junction 32 and take the A470 to Merthyr Tydfil. Go onto the A465 and follow the brown tourist
signs for the railway.

BREDGAR & WORMSHILL LIGHT RAILWAY

Address: The Warren, Bredgar,
near Sittingbourne, Kent   ME9 8AT
Telephone Nº: (01622) 884254
Year Formed: 1972
Location of Line: 1 mile south of Bredgar
Gauge: 1 foot 11¾ inches
Length of Line: ½ mile

Nº of Steam Locos: 13
Nº of Other Locos: 1
Nº of Members: –
Annual Membership Fee: –
Approx Nº of Visitors P.A.: 5,000

GENERAL INFORMATION

Nearest Railtrack Station:
Hollingbourne (3 miles) or Sittingbourne (5 miles)
Nearest Bus Station: Sittingbourne
Car Parking: 500 spaces available – free parking
Coach Parking: Free parking available by appointment
Souvenir Shop(s): Yes
Food & Drinks: Yes

SPECIAL INFORMATION

A small but beautiful railway in rural Kent. The
railway also has other attractions including Traction
Engines, a working Beam Engine, Vintage cars, a
Locomotive Shed, a picnic site and woodland walks.

OPERATING INFORMATION

Opening Times: Open on the first Sunday of the
month from May to September. Also Enthusiasts
Day on 23rd June. Open from 10.30am to 5.00pm
Steam Working: 11.00am to 4.30pm
Prices: Adult £5.00
Child £2.50

Detailed Directions by Car:
Take the M20 and exit at Junction 8 (Leeds Castle exit). Travel 4½ miles due north through Hollingbourne. The
Railway is situated a little over 1 mile south of Bredgar village.

BRESSINGHAM STEAM EXPERIENCE

Address: Bressingham Steam Museum, Bressingham, Diss, Norfolk IP22 2AB	**Nº of Steam Locos**: Many Steam locos
Telephone Nº: (01379) 687386	**Nº of Other Locos**: –
Year Formed: Mid 50's	**Nº of Members**: 100 volunteers
Location of Line: Bressingham, Near Diss	**Annual Membership Fee**: –
Length of Line: 5 miles in total (3 lines)	**Approx Nº of Visitors P.A.**: 100,000+
	Gauge: Standard & 3 Narrow gauge lines

GENERAL INFORMATION

Nearest Railtrack Station: Diss (2½ miles)
Nearest Bus Station: Bressingham (1¼ miles)
Car Parking: Free parking for 400 cars available
Coach Parking: Free parking for 30 coaches
Souvenir Shop(s): Yes
Food & Drinks: Yes

SPECIAL INFORMATION

In addition to Steam locomotives, Bressingham has a large selection of steam traction engines, fixed steam engines and also the National Dad's Army Museum, two extensive gardens and a water garden centre.

Web site: www.bressingham.co.uk

OPERATING INFORMATION

Opening Times: Daily from 23rd March to the end of September 10.30am to 5.30pm. Daily in October from 10.30 to 4.30pm.
Steam Working: All days, but 'Full Steam' days on Thursdays and Sundays have more trains and steam demonstrations running.
Prices: Adult £10.00
　　　　　　Child £8.00
　　　　　　Family £35.00
　　　　　　Senior Citizens & Students £9.00
A Family Season Ticket is available for £55.00 – please contact Bressingham for further information.

Detailed Directions by Car:
From All Parts: Take the A11 to Thetford and then follow the A1066 towards Diss for Bressingham. The Museum is signposted by the brown tourist signs.

BRISTOL HARBOUR RAILWAY

Address: Bristol Industrial Museum, Princes Wharf, City Docks, Bristol, BS1 4RN **Telephone Nº:** (0117) 925-1470 **Year Formed:** 1978 **Location of Line:** South side of the Floating Harbour	**Length of Line:** 1½ miles **Nº of Steam Locos:** 2 **Nº of Other Locos:** 1 **Nº of Members:** – **Annual Membership Fee:** – **Approx Nº of Visitors P.A.:** 70,000 **Gauge:** Standard

GENERAL INFORMATION

Nearest Railtrack Station: Bristol Temple Meads (1 mile)
Nearest Bus Station: City Centre (½ mile)
Car Parking: Parking available at site
Coach Parking: Drop off and Pick up only
Souvenir Shop(s): Yes
Food & Drinks: Cafes available near the Railway

SPECIAL INFORMATION

The Railway is one of the attractions of the Bristol Industrial Museum which has over 400 exhibits to see, housed in historic transit sheds by a dockside location.

OPERATING INFORMATION

Opening Times: Saturday to Wednesday between 25th March & 29th October. Weekends only November to March. Opens from 10.00am – 5.00pm
Steam Working: 2002 dates: March 23/24/30/31; April 1/13/14/20/21; May 4/5/6/18/19; June 1/2/3/4/15/16/29/30; July 13/14/27/28; August 24/25/26; September 14/15/21/22; October 5/6/19/20/26/27
Prices: Adult £1.00
            Child 60p
N.B. Admission to the Museum is free of charge.

Detailed Directions by Car:
From All Parts: Follow signs to Bristol City Centre and then the Brown Tourist signs for the Museum. A good landmark to look out for are the 4 huge quayside cranes.

BUCKINGHAMSHIRE RAILWAY CENTRE

Address: Quainton Road Station, Quainton, Aylesbury, Bucks. HP22 4BY
Telephone Nº: (01296) 655720
Year Formed: 1969
Location of Line: At Quainton on the old Metropolitan/Great Central Line
Length of Line: 2 × ½ mile demo tracks

Nº of Steam Locos: 35
Nº of Other Locos: 6
Nº of Members: 1,000
Annual Membership Fee: £12.00
Approx Nº of Visitors P.A.: 40,000
Gauge: Standard
Recorded Info. Line: (01296) 655450

GENERAL INFORMATION

Nearest Railtrack Station: Aylesbury (6 miles)
Nearest Bus Station: Aylesbury
Car Parking: Free parking for 500 cars available
Coach Parking: Free parking for 30 coaches
Souvenir Shop(s): Yes
Food & Drinks: Yes

SPECIAL INFORMATION

In addition to a large collection of locomotives and carriages, the Centre has an extensive outdoor miniature railway system.
Web site: www.bucksrailcentre.org.uk

OPERATING INFORMATION

Opening Times: Wednesday to Sunday and Bank Holidays from March to October. Open from 10.30am to 4.30pm.
Steam Working: Sundays and Bank Holidays from April to October and also on Wednesdays during the School holidays.
Prices: Adult £6.00
 Child £5.00
 (Under 5's Free of charge)
 Senior Citizen £5.00
 Family £18.00
 (2 adults + up to 4 children)

Detailed Directions by Car:
The Buckinghamshire Railway Centre is signposted off the A41 Aylesbury to Bicester Road at Waddesdon and off the A413 Buckingham to Aylesbury road at Whitchurch. Junctions 7, 8 and 9 of the M40 are all close by.

BURE VALLEY RAILWAY

Address: Aylsham Station, Norwich Road, Aylsham, Norfolk NR11 6BW
Telephone Nº: (01263) 733858
Year Formed: 1989
Location of Line: Between Aylsham & Wroxham
Length of Line: 9 miles

Nº of Steam Locos: 5
Nº of Other Locos: 3
Approx Nº of Visitors P.A.: 127,000
Gauge: 15 inches
Web Site: www.bvrw.co.uk
e-mail: info@bvrw.co.uk

GENERAL INFORMATION

Nearest Railtrack Station: Wroxham (adjacent)
Nearest Bus Station: Aylsham (bus passes station)
Car Parking: Free parking at Aylsham & Wroxham Stations
Coach Parking: As above
Souvenir Shop(s): Yes at both Stations
Food & Drinks: Yes (also a Restaurant at Aylsham)

SPECIAL INFORMATION

Boat trains connect at Wroxham with 1½ hour cruise on the Norfolk Broads. Steam Locomotive driving courses are available in off-peak periods.

OPERATING INFORMATION

Opening Times: Various dates from 24th March to the 27th October. Daily in July and August. Closed Fridays & Saturdays in May & June. Trains run from 10.15am to 5.15pm most days when open.
Steam Working: Most trains are steam hauled
Prices: Adult Return £7.50 (Single £4.50)
Child Return £4.20 (Single £3.00)
Senior Cit. Return £7.00 (Single £4.00)
Family Return £21.00 (2 adult + 2 child)

Some Carriages have special facilities to carry wheelchairs. Party discounts are available for groups of 20+ if booked in advance.

Detailed Directions by Car:
From Norwich: Aylsham Station is midway between Norwich and Cromer on the A140 – follow the Aylsham Town Centre signs. Wroxham Station is adjacent to the Wroxham British Rail Station – take the A1151 from Norwich; From King's Lynn: Take A148 and B1354 to reach Aylsham Station.

CADEBY LIGHT RAILWAY

Address: The Old Rectory, Cadeby, Nuneaton, Warks. CV13 0AS
Telephone N°: (01455) 290462
Year Formed: 1961
Location of Line: 1 mile from Market Bosworth, 6 miles from Hinckley
Length of Line: 75 yards

N° of Steam Locos: 3
N° of Other Locos: 15
N° of Members: –
Annual Membership Fee: –
Approx N° of Visitors P.A.: –
Gauge: 2 feet

GENERAL INFORMATION

Nearest Railtrack Station: Hinckley (6 miles)
Nearest Bus Station: Market Bosworth (1 mile)
Car Parking: Free parking at site
Coach Parking: Roadside parking
Souvenir Shop(s): Yes
Food & Drinks: Yes

SPECIAL INFORMATION

A new museum was opened in 1990, 'The Boston Collection', encompassing the lifetime collection of the late Reverend Teddy Boston and his family. The narrow gauge railway running in the grounds of the old rectory has been saved by Teddy Boston's widow and a small band of dedicated supporters.

OPERATING INFORMATION

Opening Times: 2nd Saturday of selected months plus specials – please phone for details.
Steam Working: As above.
Prices: Free, but donations are requested.

Detailed Directions by Car:
Exit the M1 at Junction 18 and take the A5 to Hinckley. From Hinckley take the A447 to Cadeby.

CALEDONIAN RAILWAY

Address: The Station, 2 Park Road, Brechin, Angus   DD9 7AF
Telephone Nº: (01561) 377760
Year Formed: 1979
Location of Line: From Brechin to Bridge of Dun
Length of Line: 4 miles

Nº of Steam Locos: 3
Nº of Other Locos: 6
Nº of Members: 250
Annual Membership Fee: Adult £10.00; Family £15.00; OAP/Junior £5.00
Approx Nº of Visitors P.A.: 12,000
Gauge: Standard

GENERAL INFORMATION

Nearest Railtrack Station: Montrose (4½ miles)
Nearest Bus Station: Brechin (200 yards)
Car Parking: Ample free parking at both Stations
Coach Parking: Free parking at both Stations
Souvenir Shop(s): Yes
Food & Drinks: Light refreshments are available

SPECIAL INFORMATION

Brechin Station is the only original Terminus station in preservation.

OPERATING INFORMATION

Opening Times: Open Easter Sunday, 3 Sundays before Christmas & every Sunday from June to September. Open on other dates including Special 50th Anniversary weekend – 3rd & 4th August.
Steam Working: Steam service on every Sunday from 26th May to 8th September.
Prices: Adult Return £5.00
　　　　　　Child Return £3.00
　　　　　　Senior Citizen Return £4.00
　　　　　　Family Return £16.00 (2 adult + 3 child)
Group discounts are available if booked in advance.

Detailed Directions by Car:
From South: For Brechin Station, leave the A90 at the Brechin turn-off and go straight through the Town Centre. Pass the Northern Hotel, take the 2nd exit at the mini-roundabout then it is 150 yards to Park Road/St. Ninian Square; From North: For Brechin Station, leave the A90 at the Brechin turn-off and go straight through Trinity Village. Turn left at the mini-roundabout, it is then 250 yards to Park Road/St. Ninian Square. Bridge of Dun is situated half way between Brechin and Montrose. (Follow tourist signs).

CHASEWATER RAILWAY

Address: Chasewater Country Park, Pool Road, Near Brownhills, Staffs, WS8 7NL
Telephone N°: (01543) 452623
Year Re-formed: 1985
Location of Line: Chasewater Country Park, Brownhills, near Walsall
Length of Line: 2 miles

N° of Steam Locos: 7
N° of Other Locos: 8
N° of Members: 350
Annual Membership Fee: Adult £7.50; Family £12.50; Concessions £5.00
Approx N° of Visitors P.A.: 14,000
Gauge: Standard

GENERAL INFORMATION

Nearest Railtrack Station: Walsall or Birmingham (both approximately 8 miles)
Nearest Bus Station: Walsall or Birmingham
Car Parking: Free parking in Chasewater Park
Coach Parking: Free parking in Chasewater Park
Souvenir Shop(s): Yes
Food & Drinks: Yes

SPECIAL INFORMATION

Chasewater Railway is based on the Cannock Chase & Wolverhampton Railway opened in 1856. The railway passed into the hands of the National Coal Board which then ceased using the line in 1965. An extension to Chasetown and a new station at Chasewater Heaths opens on Easter Sunday, 2002.

OPERATING INFORMATION

Opening Times: Sundays & Bank Holidays from 31st March to the end of October + Santa Specials.
Steam Working: 11.30am, 12.50pm, 2.10pm, 3.30pm and 4.50pm.
Prices: Adult Return £2.45
Child Return £2.45
Family Return £6.45
All tickets offer unlimited rides on the day of issue. The replica locomotive 'Sans Pareil' will be operating services on 2nd, 3rd, 9th, 16th and 23rd June 2002.

Detailed Directions by Car:
Chasewater Country Park is situated in Brownhills off the A5 southbound near the junction of the A5 with the A452 Chester Road. Follow the Brown tourist signs on the A5 for the Country Park.

CHINNOR & PRINCES RISBOROUGH RAILWAY

Address: Station Road, Chinnor, Oxon	**Nº of Steam Locos**: 1
Telephone Nº: (01844) 353535 (timetable)	**Nº of Other Locos**: 3
Year Formed: 1989	**Nº of Members**: 650
Location of Line: The Icknield Line,	**Annual Membership Fee**: Adult £11.00;
Princes Risborough	Family £16.50; Children & OAP £5.00
Length of Line: 3½ miles	**Approx Nº of Visitors P.A.**: 15,000
Gauge: Standard	**Web Site**: http://www.cprra.co.uk

GENERAL INFORMATION

Nearest Railtrack Station: Princes Risborough (4 miles)
Nearest Bus Station: High Wycombe (10 miles)
Car Parking: Free parking at site
Coach Parking: Prior arrangement preferred but not necessary
Souvenir Shop(s): Yes
Food & Drinks: Soft drinks and light snacks in Station Buffet. Buffet usually available on trains.

SPECIAL INFORMATION

The Chinnor & Princes Risborough Railway operates the remaining 3½ mile section of the former GWR Watlington Branch from Chinnor to Thame Junction.

OPERATING INFORMATION

Opening Times: Most Saturdays and all Sundays from April to October + Santa Specials.
Steam Working: Operates from 10.00am to 5.00pm on Peak Season Sundays.
Prices: Adult Return £5.00
Child Return £3.00
Family Return £13.00
(2 adults + 2 children)
Senior Citizen Return £4.00

Detailed Directions by Car:
From All Parts: The railway at Chinnor is situated in Station Road just off the B4009. Junction 6 of the M40 is 3 miles away and Princes Risborough 5 miles further along the B4009. Once in Chinnor follow the brown Tourist signs to the railway.

CHOLSEY & WALLINGFORD RAILWAY

Address: P.O. Box 16, St. John's Road, Wallingford, Oxon OX10 0NF
Telephone Nº: (01491) 835067 (24hr info)
Year Formed: 1981
Location of Line: Wallingford, Oxon.
Length of Line: 2½ miles

Nº of Steam Locos: 1 (+ visiting Locos)
Nº of Other Locos: 4
Nº of Members: 250
Annual Membership Fee: £10.00
Approx Nº of Visitors P.A.: 4,000
Gauge: Standard

GENERAL INFORMATION

Nearest Railtrack Station: Joint station at Cholsey
Nearest Bus Station: Wallingford (¼ mile)
Car Parking: Roadside parking available
Coach Parking: Roadside parking available
Souvenir Shop(s): Yes
Food & Drinks: Yes

SPECIAL INFORMATION

The Wallingford branch was originally intended as a through line to Princes Risborough, via Watlington, but ultimately became the first standard gauge branch of Brunel's broad-gauge London to Bristol line.

OPERATING INFORMATION

Opening Times: Selected weekends from Easter until Christmas – phone for details.
Steam Working: Approximately 11.00am to 4.30pm
Prices: Adult Return £4.00
Child Return £3.00
Family Return £12.00 (2 adult + 2 child)
N.B. Prices are subject to change for Thomas the Tank Engine events and Santa Specials.

Detailed Directions by Car:
From All Parts: Exit from the A34 at the Milton Interchange (between E. Ilsley and Abingdon). Follow signs to Didcot and Wallingford. Take Wallingford bypass, then turn left at the first roundabout (signposted Hithercroft Estate). The Station is then ½ mile on the right.

CHURNET VALLEY RAILWAY

Address: The Railway Station, Cheddleton, Leek, Staffs. ST13 7EE	**Nº of Steam Locos:** 3
Telephone Nº: (01538) 360522	**Nº of Other Locos:** 3
Year Formed: 1978	**Nº of Members:** –
Location of Line: Cheddleton to Froghall	**Annual Membership Fee:** £15.00
Length of Line: 5½ miles	**Approx Nº of Visitors P.A.:** 30,000 plus
	Gauge: Standard

GENERAL INFORMATION

Nearest Railtrack Station: Stoke-on-Trent (12 miles)

Nearest Bus Station: Leek (5 miles)

Car Parking: Parking available on site

Coach Parking: Restricted space – please book in advance

Souvenir Shop(s): Yes

Food & Drinks: Yes

SPECIAL INFORMATION

An extension of the line was opened in 2001 and work is to commence on a new station in Spring 2002.

OPERATING INFORMATION

Opening Times: Steam trains run from Easter to the end of September every Sunday and Bank Holiday Monday. Also on every Wednesday in August and every Saturday during July & August.

Steam Working: 11.00am to 4.50pm on Sundays & Wednesdays in August.

Prices: Please telephone (01538) 360522 for details.

Detailed Directions by Car:

From All Parts: Take the M6 to Stoke-on-Trent and follow trunk roads to Leek. Cheddleton Station is just off the A520 Leek to Stone road. Frogmore Station is just off the A52 Ashbourne Road.

CLEETHORPES COAST LIGHT RAILWAY

Address: King's Road, Cleethorpes, North East Lincolnshire DN35 0AG	**No of Steam Locos**: 5
Telephone No: (01472) 604657	**No of Other Locos**: 4
Year Formed: 1948	**No of Members**: 65
Location of Line: Lakeside Park & Marine embankment along Cleethorpes seafront	**Annual Membership Fee**: £5.50
	Approx No of Visitors P.A.: 106,000
Length of Line: 1¼ miles	**Gauge**: 15 inches
	E-mail: genoff@cclrltd.freeserve.co.uk

GENERAL INFORMATION

Nearest Railtrack Station: Cleethorpes (1 mile)
Nearest Bus Stop: Meridian Point (opposite)
Car Parking: Boating Lake car park – 500 spaces (fee charged)
Coach Parking: As above
Souvenir Shop(s): Yes
Food & Drinks: Brief Encounters Tearoom on Lakeside Station

SPECIAL INFORMATION

Visiting engines will attend at various times during the year. Phone for further details.

OPERATING INFORMATION

Opening Times: Open daily from 9th April to 22nd April then daily from 20th May to 9th September. Weekends, Bank holidays and school holidays at all other times. Open 11.00am to dusk in Winter, 6.00pm in Summer.
Steam Working: Weekends throughout the year
Prices: Adult Return £2.00
  Child Return £1.50
  Family Return £6.00

Detailed Directions by Car:
Take the M180 to the A180 and continue to its' end. Follow signs for Cleethorpes. The Railway is situated along Cleethorpes seafront 1 mile south of the Pier. Look for the brown Railway Engine tourist signs and the main station is adjacent to the Leisure Centre.

COLNE VALLEY RAILWAY

Address: Castle Hedingham Station, Yeldham Road, Castle Hedingham, Essex, CO9 3DZ	**Length of Line:** Approximately 1 mile
Telephone Nº: (01787) 461174	**Nº of Steam Locos:** 10
Year Formed: 1974	**Nº of Other Locos:** 11
Location of Line: On A1017, 7 miles north-west of Braintree	**Nº of Members:** 250
	Annual Membership Fee: £11.00
	Approx Nº of Visitors P.A.: 45,000
	Gauge: Standard

GENERAL INFORMATION

Nearest Railtrack Station: Braintree (7 miles)
Nearest Bus Station: Hedingham bus from Braintree stops at the Railway (except on Sundays)
Car Parking: Free parking at site
Coach Parking: Free parking at site
Souvenir Shop(s): Yes
Food & Drinks: Yes – on operational days. Also Pullman Sunday Lunches – bookings necessary.

SPECIAL INFORMATION

The railway is being re-built on a section of the old Colne Valley & Halstead Railway, with all buildings, bridges, signal boxes, etc. re-located on site. The Railway also has a Farm Park to visit on site.

OPERATING INFORMATION

Opening Times: Trains run every Sunday and Bank Holiday from 10th March to the end of October. Also daily during the School Summer holidays. The Railway is open daily (sometimes without trains running) from 1st April to 23rd December 11.00am to 5.00pm.
Steam Working: Sundays 12.00pm to 4.00pm. Also Wednesdays & Thursdays in School summer holidays.
Prices: Adult – Steam days £6; Diesel days £5.00; Static days £3.00
Child – Steam £3.00; Diesel £2.50; Static £1.50
Family (2 adults + 4 children) – Steam £16.50; Diesel £12.50; Static £7.50

Detailed Directions by Car:
The Railway is situated on the A1017 between Halstead and Haverhill, 7 miles north-west of Braintree.

CONWY VALLEY RAILWAY MUSEUM

Address: Old Goods Yard, Betws-y-Coed, Conwy, North Wales LL24 0AL	**No of Steam Locos**: 4
Telephone No: (01690) 710568	**No of Other Locos**: 2
Year Formed: 1983	**No of Members**: –
Location of Line: Betws-y-Coed	**Annual Membership Fee**: –
Length of Line: One and an eighth miles	**Approx No of Visitors P.A.**: 50,000
	Gauge: 7¼ inches and 15 inches

GENERAL INFORMATION

Nearest Railtrack Station: Betws-y-Coed (20 yards)
Nearest Bus Station: 40 yards
Car Parking: Car park at site
Coach Parking: Car park at site
Souvenir Shop(s): Yes
Food & Drinks: Yes – Buffet Coach Cafe

SPECIAL INFORMATION

The Museum houses the unique 3D dioramas by the late Jack Nelson. Also the ¼ size steam loco 'Britannia'.

OPERATING INFORMATION

Opening Times: Daily from March to the end of October 10.15am to 5.00pm. Open daily in the Winter from 10.15am to 4.00pm.
Trains Working: Daily from 10.15am
Prices: Adult – £1 entry to museum; Train £1.00; Tram 80p
Child/OAP – 50p entry to museum; Train £1.00; Tram 80p
Family tickets – £2.50

Detailed Directions by Car:
From Midlands & South: Take M54/M6 onto the A5 and into Betws-y-Coed; From Other Parts: Take the A55 coast road then the A470 to Betws-y-Coed. The museum is located by the Railtrack Station directly off the A5.

CRICH – NATIONAL TRAMWAY MUSEUM

Address: Crich Tramway Village, Crich, Matlock, Derbyshire DE4 5DP
Telephone Nº: (0870) 7587267
Year Formed: 1964
Location of Line: Crich
Length of Line: 1 mile

Nº of Steam Locos: None
Nº of Other Locos: 50 trams approx.
Nº of Members: 2,500
Annual Membership Fee: £16.00
Approx Nº of Visitors P.A.: 90,000
Web site: www.tramway.co.uk

GENERAL INFORMATION

Nearest Railtrack Station: Whatstandwell (1 mile)
Nearest Bus Station: Crich
Car Parking: Free parking available on site
Coach Parking: Free parking available on site
Souvenir Shop(s): Yes
Food & Drinks: Yes

SPECIAL INFORMATION

The admission price includes unlimited tram rides plus a host of indoor attractions.

OPERATING INFORMATION

Opening Times: 10.00am to 5.30pm daily from April to October. Open at Weekends in winter.
Steam Working: On certain "Day out with Thomas" events only – see pages 10 & 11.
Prices: Adult £7.00
Child £3.50
Family Tickets £19.00

Detailed Directions by Car:
From All Parts: The Museum is situated just of the B5035 near Crich – this is approximately 15 miles north of Derby. Exit the M1 at Junction 28 if travelling from the North or Junction 26 from the South.

Darlington Railway Centre & Museum

Address: North Road Station, Darlington, Co. Durham   DL3 6ST
Telephone Nº: (01325) 460532
Year Formed: 1975
Location of Line: Adjacent to North Road Station
Length of Line: ¼ mile

Nº of Steam Locos: 7
Nº of Other Locos: –
Nº of Members: –
Annual Membership Fee: –
Approx Nº of Visitors P.A.: 22,000
Gauge: Standard

GENERAL INFORMATION

Nearest Railtrack Station: North Road (adjacent)
Nearest Bus Station: Darlington (1 mile)
Car Parking: Free parking at site
Coach Parking: Free parking at site
Souvenir Shop(s): Yes
Food & Drinks: Yes – Cafe in the Summer, drinks and confectionery at other times.

SPECIAL INFORMATION

The museum is an 1842 station on the route of the Stockton and Darlington Railway and is devoted to the Railways of north-east England.

OPERATING INFORMATION

Opening Times: The Museum is open 10.00am to 5.00pm daily, although it is closed during January. The Locomotive Works run by the A1 Steam Locomotive Trust is open 11.00am to 4.00pm on Saturdays.
Prices: Adult – £2.10
                Child – £1.05

Detailed Directions by Car:
From Darlington Town Centre: Follow the A167 north for about ¾ mile then turn left immediately before the Railway bridge; From A1(M): Exit at Junction 59 then follow A167 towards Darlington and turn right after passing under the Railway bridge.

DEAN FOREST RAILWAY

Address: Norchard Centre, Forest Road; Lydney, Gloucestershire   GL15 4ET
Telephone Nº: (01594) 845840
Information Line: (01594) 843423 (24 hr.)
Year Formed: 1970
Location of Line: Lydney, Gloucestershire
Length of Line: 3 miles

Nº of Steam Locos: 8 (2 working)
Nº of Other Locos: 2
Nº of Members: 850
Annual Membership Fee: Adult £12.00; Family (4 persons) £15.00
Approx Nº of Visitors P.A.: 55,000
Gauge: Standard

GENERAL INFORMATION

Nearest Railtrack Station: Lydney (200 metres)
Nearest Bus Station: Lydney (1 mile)
Car Parking: 600 spaces available at Norchard
Coach Parking: Ample space available
Souvenir Shop(s): Yes + a Museum
Food & Drinks: Yes – on operational days only

SPECIAL INFORMATION

Dean Forest Railway preserves the sole surviving line of the Severn and Wye Railway. The Railway is lengthening the line to a total of four miles.
A section north of Norchard to Tufts (1 mile) is now worked by DMU from Lydney Junction giving a round trip of 10 miles.

OPERATING INFORMATION

Opening Times: Sundays & Bank Holidays from 24th March to 27th October. Also Wednesdays June to the end of September and Thursdays and Saturdays in August. 'Days out with Thomas' (the Tank Engine) are 1st to 5th June and 29th August to 1st September. Santa Specials run during December.
Steam Working: Trains depart Norchard at 11.30am, 12.30pm, 1.30pm, 2.30pm and 3.30pm.
Prices: Adult Return £5.50
          Child Return £3.50 (ages 5-16 years old)
          Senior Citizens £4.50
N.B. Fares may differ on special dates.

Detailed Directions by Car:
From M50 & Ross-on-Wye: Take the B4228 and B4234 via Coleford to reach Lydney. Norchard is located on the B4234, ¾ mile north of Lydney Town Centre; From Monmouth: Take the A4136 and B4431 onto the B4234 via Coleford; From South Wales: Take the M4 then M48 onto the A48 via Chepstow to Lydney; From Midlands/ Gloucester: Take the M5 to Gloucester then the A48 to Lydney; From the West Country: Take the M4 and M48 via the 'Old' Severn Bridge to Chepstow and then the A48 to Lydney.

DERWENT VALLEY LIGHT RAILWAY

Address: Murton Park, Murton Lane, Murton, York   YO19 5UF
Telephone Nº: (01904) 489966
Year Formed: 1991
Location of Line: Murton, near York
Length of Line: ½ mile

Nº of Steam Locos: 2
Nº of Other Locos: 5
Nº of Members: 200
Annual Membership Fee: £8.00
Approx Nº of Visitors P.A.: 10,000
Gauge: Standard

GENERAL INFORMATION

Nearest Railtrack Station: York (4 miles)
Nearest Bus Station: York (4 miles)
Car Parking: Large free car park at the site
Coach Parking: Free at the site
Souvenir Shop(s): Yes – at the Yorkshire Museum of Farming (same site)
Food & Drinks: Yes – as above

SPECIAL INFORMATION

The site is the remnants of the Derwent Valley Railway which was the last privately owned railway in England, originally opened in 1913.

OPERATING INFORMATION

Opening Times: Sundays and Bank Holidays from Easter until the end of September. Also Santa Specials run in December.
Steam Working: Last Sunday in the month and Bank Holidays – 10.00am to 5.00pm.
Prices: Adult £3.00
　　　　　Child £1.50

Prices are for entrance to the Yorkshire Museum of Farming – train rides are included in the price.

Detailed Directions by Car:
From All Parts: The railway is well signposted for the Yorkshire Museum of Farming from the A64 (York to Scarborough road), the A1079 (York to Hull road) and the A166 (York to Bridlington road).

DIDCOT RAILWAY CENTRE

Address: Didcot Railway Centre, Didcot, Oxfordshire OX11 7NJ **Telephone N°:** (01235) 817200 **Year Formed:** 1961 **Location of Line:** Didcot **Length of Line:** ¾ mile **Gauge:** Standard	**N° of Steam Locos:** 23 **N° of Other Locos:** 2 **N° of Members:** 4,100 **Annual Membership Fee:** Full £18.00; Over 60/Under 18 £10.00; Family £24.00 **Approx N° of Visitors P.A.:** 70,000 **Web Site:** www.didcotrailwaycentre.org.uk

GENERAL INFORMATION

Nearest Railtrack Station: Didcot Parkway (adjacent)
Nearest Bus Station: Buses to Didcot call at the Railway station
Car Parking: BR car park adjacent
Coach Parking: Further details on application
Souvenir Shop(s): Yes
Food & Drinks: Yes

SPECIAL INFORMATION

The Centre is based on a Great Western Railway engine shed and is devoted to the re-creation of part of the GWR.

OPERATING INFORMATION

Opening Times: Weekends all year round, open daily from 23rd March to 29th September. 10.00am to 5.00pm (10.00am to 4.00pm in the Winter).
Steam Working: First & last Sundays of each month. Bank Holidays, all Sundays July & August, all Wednesdays 17th July to 28th August. Also on Saturdays in August.
Prices: Adult £4.00 – £8.00 (including rides)
Child £3.00 – £6.50 (including rides)
Discounted family tickets are often available (2 adults + 2 children).
Prices vary depending on the events.

Detailed Directions by Car:
From East & West: Take the M4 to Junction 13 then the A34 and A4130 (follow brown Tourist signs to Didcot Railway Centre); From North: The centre is signed from the A34 to A4130.

DOBWALLS FAMILY ADVENTURE PARK

Address: Dobwalls Family Adventure Park, near Liskeard, Cornwall PL14 6HB
Telephone Nº: (01579) 320325/321129
Year Formed: 1970
Location of Line: Near Liskeard, Cornwall
Length of Line: 2 × 1 mile tracks

Nº of Steam Locos: 6
Nº of Other Locos: 4
Nº of Members: –
Annual Membership Fee: –
Gauge: 7¼ inches
Web site: www.dobwallsadventurepark.co.uk

GENERAL INFORMATION
Nearest Railtrack Station: Liskeard (3 miles)
Nearest Bus Station: Most National Express Coaches travel through Dobwalls.
Car Parking: Ample parking available at site
Coach Parking: Large coach park available
Souvenir Shop(s): Yes
Food & Drinks: Yes

SPECIAL INFORMATION
Formerly known as the Forest Railroad Park, Dobwalls has a large number of other attractions including many for children. There is also a craft centre and art gallery.

OPERATING INFORMATION
Opening Times: Open most days from Easter until the end of October. Opens from 10.30am to 5.00pm.
Steam Working: All days when open
Prices: Children under the age of 2 – Free
Single person ticket – £6.95
2 person ticket – £13.50
3 person ticket – £20.00
4 person ticket – £26.00
Disabled & Senior Citizens – £5.50

Detailed Directions by Car:
From All Parts: Dobwalls Family Adventure Park is situated just off the A38 at Dobwalls village, 3 miles from Liskeard.

DOWNPATRICK RAILWAY MUSEUM

Address: Market Street, Downpatrick, Co. Down, Northern Ireland
Telephone Nº: (028) 4461-5779
Year Formed: 1985
Location of Line: Downpatrick
Length of Line: 1 mile
Gauge: Standard

Nº of Steam Locos: 3
Nº of Other Locos: 5
Nº of Members: 180
Annual Membership Fee: Adult £15.00, Family £20.00, Concessions £10.00
Approx Nº of Visitors P.A.: 13,000

GENERAL INFORMATION

Nearest Railtrack Station: –
Nearest Bus Station: Adjacent to Station
Car Parking: Ample parking adjacent to Station
Coach Parking: Ample parking adjacent to Station
Souvenir Shop(s): Yes
Food & Drinks: Yes

SPECIAL INFORMATION

Footplate experience courses run on Saturdays from July to September at a price of £ 100.00.

OPERATING INFORMATION

Opening Times: The Museum is open daily from June to September.
Steam Working: Saturdays and Sundays in July, August and also first 2 Sundays in September. Trains are usually steam hauled and run from 2.00pm to 5.00pm. Special trains run at Easter, Halloween and Christmas.
Prices: Adult £3.60
Child £2.60

Detailed Directions by Car:
From Belfast take the A7 Downpatrick Road. Upon arrival in Downpatrick, follow the brown tourist signs and the Railway Museum is adjacent to the bus station.

EAST ANGLIAN RAILWAY MUSEUM

Address: Chappel & Wakes Colne Station, Colchester, Essex   CO6 2DS
Telephone Nº: (01206) 242524
Year Formed: 1969
Location of Line: 8 miles south of Colchester on Marks Tey to Sudbury branch
Length of Line: A third of a mile

Nº of Steam Locos: 5
Nº of Other Locos: 6
Nº of Members: 750
Annual Membership Fee: Adult £17.50; Senior Citizen £12.50
Approx Nº of Visitors P.A.: 40,000
Gauge: Standard

GENERAL INFORMATION

Nearest Railtrack Station: Chappel & Wakes Colne (adajcent)
Nearest Bus Station: Chappel (500 yards)
Car Parking: Free parking at site
Coach Parking: Free parking at site
Souvenir Shop(s): Yes
Food & Drinks: Yes – all weekends & every day in the summer.

SPECIAL INFORMATION

The museum has the most comprehensive collection of railway architecture & engineering in the region.

OPERATING INFORMATION

Opening Times: Open daily 10.00am to 5.00pm. Steam days open from 11.00am to 5.00pm
Steam Working: Steam days are the 1st Sunday monthly from April to August and also in October. Bank Holidays are also Steam days.
Prices: Adult £3.00 non-Steam; £6.00 Steam
Child £2.00 non-Steam; £3.00 Steam
O.A.P. £2.50 non-Steam; £4.50 Steam
Family £8.00 non-Steam; £15.00 Steam
Children under the age of 4 are admitted free of charge. A 10% discount is available for bookings for more than 10 people.

Detailed Directions by Car:
From North & South: Turn off the A12 south west of Colchester onto the A1124 (formerly the A604). The Museum is situated just off the A1124; From West: Turn off the A120 just before Marks Tey (signposted).

EASTBOURNE MINIATURE STEAM RAILWAY

Address: Lottbridge Drove, Eastbourne, East Sussex BN23 6NS	**Nº of Steam Locos:** 5
Telephone Nº: (01323) 520229	**Nº of Other Locos:** 2
Year Formed: 1992	**Nº of Members:** –
Location of Line: Eastbourne	**Approx Nº of Visitors P.A.:** –
Length of Line: 1 mile	**Gauge:** 7¼ inches
	Web site: www.emsr.co.uk

GENERAL INFORMATION

Nearest Railtrack Station: Eastbourne (2 miles)
Nearest Bus Station: Eastbourne (2 miles)
Car Parking: Free parking on site
Coach Parking: Free parking on site
Souvenir Shop(s): Yes
Food & Drinks: Yes

SPECIAL INFORMATION

The Railway site also has many other attractions including model railways, an adventure playground, nature walk, maze and picnic area.

OPERATING INFORMATION

Opening Times: Open 10.00am to 5.00pm daily from 23rd March to 30th September. Also special events on Easter Sunday and Bonfire Night.
Steam Working: Weekends, Bank Holidays and during School Holidays. Diesel at other times.
Prices: Adult £3.95
Child £3.45 (2 years and under free)
Family Tickets £14.00
(2 adults + 2 children)

Detailed Directions by Car:
From All Parts: Travel to Eastbourne and follow the signs for 'Eastbourne Industrial Estates'. Follow the Brown tourist signs for the 'Mini Railway'.

EAST KENT LIGHT RAILWAY

Address: Station Road, Shepherdswell, Dover, Kent   CT15 7PD
Telephone Nº: (01304) 832042
Year Formed: 1985
Location of Line: Between Shepherdswell and Eythorne
Length of Line: 2 miles

Nº of Steam Locos: 3
Nº of Other Locos: 5
Nº of Members: 400
Annual Membership Fee: £15.00 (Adult)
Approx Nº of Visitors P.A.: 15,000
Gauge: Standard and also 5 inch and 3¼ inch miniature gauge

GENERAL INFORMATION

Nearest Railtrack Station: Shepherdswell (Connex S.E. – 50 yards)
Nearest Bus Station: Dover
Car Parking: Available Shepherdswell and Eythorne
Coach Parking: In adjacent Station Yard
Souvenir Shop(s): Yes
Food & Drinks: Yes

SPECIAL INFORMATION

The East Kent Railway was originally built between 1911 and 1917 to service Tilmanstone Colliery.

Closed in the mid-1980's, the railway was re-opened in 1995.

OPERATING INFORMATION

Opening Times: Open weekends and Thursdays throughout the year for static viewing. Trains run: During Easter and Sundays from June to September; Saturdays from July 13th to end of August; most weekends in December plus various other dates.
Steam Working: Most open days 11.00am to 4.00pm. Please contact the railway for details.
Prices: Adult £5.00   Child £3.50

Detailed Directions by Car:
From the A2: Take the turning to Shepherdswell and continue to the village. Pass the shop on the left and cross the railway bridge. Take the next left (Station Road) signposted at the traffic lights for the EKR; From the A256: Take the turning for Eythorne at the roundabout on the section between Eastry and Whitfield. Follow the road through Eythorne. Further on you will cross the railway line and enter Shepherdswell. After a few hundred yards take the right turn signposted for the EKR.

EAST LANCASHIRE RAILWAY

Address: Bolton Street Station, Bury, Lancashire BL9 0EY	**Nº of Steam Locos**: 14
Telephone Nº: (0161) 764-7790	**Nº of Other Locos**: 16
Year Formed: 1968	**Nº of Members**: 3,700
Location of Line: Bury to Rawtenstall	**Annual Membership Fee**: £12.00
Length of Line: 8 miles	**Approx Nº of Visitors P.A.**: 110,000
	Gauge: Standard

GENERAL INFORMATION

Nearest Railtrack Station: Manchester (then Metro Link to Bury)
Nearest Bus Station: ¼ mile
Car Parking: Adjacent
Coach Parking: Adjacent
Souvenir Shop(s): Yes
Food & Drinks: Yes

SPECIAL INFORMATION

Originally opened in 1846, the East Lancashire Railway was re-opened in 1991.

OPERATING INFORMATION

Opening Times: Every weekend & Bank Holiday 9.00am to 5.00pm
Steam Working: Most trains are steam-hauled. Saturdays alternate Steam & Diesel. 2 engines in steam on Sundays.
Prices: Adult Return £6.50
  Child Return £4.00
  Family Return £17.00
Cheaper fares are available for shorter journeys.

Detailed Directions by Car:
From All Parts: Exit the M66 at Junction 2 and take the A56 into Bury. Follow the brown tourist signs and turn right into Bolton Street at the junction with the A58. The station is about 150 yards on the right.

EASTLEIGH LAKESIDE RAILWAY

Address: Lakeside Country Park, Wide Lane, Eastleigh, Hants. SO50 5PE	**N° of Steam Locos**: 8
	N° of Other Locos: 3
Telephone N°: (023) 8063-6612	**N° of Members**: –
Year Formed: 1991	**Approx N° of Visitors P.A.**: 50,000
Location: Opposite Southampton airport	**Gauge**: 10¼ inches and 7¼ inches
Length of Line: 1¼ miles	**Web site**: www.steamtrain.co.uk

GENERAL INFORMATION

Nearest Railtrack Station: Southampton Airport (Parkway) (¼ mile)
Nearest Bus Station: Eastleigh (1½ miles)
Car Parking: Free parking available on site
Coach Parking: Free parking available on site
Souvenir Shop(s): Yes
Food & Drinks: Yes

SPECIAL INFORMATION

The railway also has a playground and picnic area overlooking the lakes.

OPERATING INFORMATION

Opening Times: Weekends throughout the year and daily during School holidays. Santa Specials run at times in September. Open 10.30am to 4.30pm.
Steam Working: As above
Prices: Standard Class Single £0.80; Return £1.50
First Class Single £1.00; Return £2.00
Annual season tickets are available. Children under the age of 2 years ride free of charge.

Detailed Directions by Car:
From All Parts: Exit the M27 at Junction 5 and take the A335 to Eastleigh. The Railway is situated 1¼ miles past Southampton Airport Station.

EAST SOMERSET RAILWAY

Address: Cranmore Railway Station, Shepton Mallet, Somerset BA4 4QP	**N° of Steam Locos:** 5
Telephone N°: (01749) 880417	**N° of Other Locos:** 2
Year Formed: 1971	**N° of Members:** 480
Location of Line: Cranmore, off A361 between Frome and Shepton Mallet	**Annual Membership Fee:** Single £13.00; Couple £17.00; Family £25.00
Length of Line: 3 miles	**Approx N° of Visitors P.A.:** 40,000
	Gauge: Standard

GENERAL INFORMATION

Nearest Railtrack Station: Castle Cary (10 miles)
Nearest Bus Station: Shepton Mallet (3 miles)
Car Parking: Space for 100 cars available
Coach Parking: Available by arrangement
Souvenir Shop(s): Yes
Food & Drinks: Yes

SPECIAL INFORMATION

Footplate experience courses available – phone (01749) 880417 for further details.

OPERATING INFORMATION

Opening Times: Complex, Museum and Engine Sheds open daily except for 24th & 25th December.
Steam Working: Sundays in the Winter, weekends in April & October, weekdays in the Summer. Open daily in August and September. Santa Specials run on weekends in December. Other special events run on various dates. Open 10.00am to 4.00pm in the Winter, 10.00am to 5.30pm in the Summer.
Prices: Adult £5.75
Child £3.75
Senior Citizens £4.75
Family £16.00

Detailed Directions by Car:
From the North: Take A367/A37 to Shepton Mallet then turn left onto A361 to Frome. Carry on to Shepton Mallet and 9 miles after Frome turn left at Cranmore; From the South: Take A36 to Frome bypass then A361 to Cranmore; From the West: Take A371 from Wells to Shepton Mallet, then A361 to Frome (then as above).

ELSECAR STEAM RAILWAY

Address: Wath Road, Elsecar, Barnsley, S74 8HJ
Telephone Nº: (01226) 740203
Year Formed: –
Location of Line: Elsecar, near Barnsley
Length of Line: 1 mile

Nº of Steam Locos: 1
Nº of Other Locos: 2
Nº of Members: –
Annual Membership Fee: –
Approx Nº of Visitors P.A.: –
Gauge: Standard
Web site: www.barnsley.gov.uk

GENERAL INFORMATION

Nearest Railtrack Station: Elsecar
Nearest Bus Station: Barnsley
Car Parking: Large free car park at the site
Coach Parking: At the site
Souvenir Shop(s): Yes
Food & Drinks: Yes

SPECIAL INFORMATION

The Railway is based at the award-winning Elsecar Heritage Centre – a living history collection of displays and artifacts occupying several acres. With craft workshops and other attractions, it is a great day out.

OPERATING INFORMATION

Opening Times: Daily from 10.00am to 5.00pm throughout the year except from 25th December to 2nd January.
Steam Working: Sundays hourly from 12.00pm to 4.00pm and on special event days – phone for details.
Prices: Adult £2.50
Senior Citizens/Under 13's £1.00
Admission to the museum and site is free of charge but donations are always welcome.

Detailed Directions by Car:
From All Parts: Exit the M1 at Junction 36 and follow the brown 'Elsecar Heritage' signs taking the A6135 for approximately 2 miles. Turn left onto Broad Carr Road for just under a mile, then right onto Armroyd Lane and right again onto Fitzwilliam Street. Free visitor car parking is available on Wentworth Road off the junction of Fitzwilliam Street and Wath Road.

EMBSAY & BOLTON ABBEY STEAM RAILWAY

Address: Bolton Abbey Station, Bolton Abbey, Skipton, N. Yorkshire BD23 6AF
Telephone Nº: (01756) 710614
Year Formed: 1968
Location of Line: 2 miles east of Skipton
Length of Line: 4½ miles

Nº of Steam Locos: 21
Nº of Other Locos: 11
Nº of Members: 700
Annual Membership Fee: £10.00
Approx Nº of Visitors P.A.: 103,000
Gauge: Standard

GENERAL INFORMATION

Nearest Railtrack Station: Skipton (2 miles), Ilkley (3 miles)
Nearest Bus Station: Skipton (2 miles), Ilkley (3 mls)
Car Parking: Large car park at both Stations
Coach Parking: Large coach park at both Stations
Souvenir Shop(s): Yes
Food & Drinks: Yes – Cafe + Buffet cars

SPECIAL INFORMATION

The line extension to Bolton Abbey has now opened.

Web site: www.embsayboltonabbeyrailway.org.uk

OPERATING INFORMATION

Opening Times: Every Sunday throughout the year. Weekends from April to the end of October and daily in the summer season.
Steam Working: Trains depart Embsay Station at 10.30am, 12.00pm, 1.30pm, 3.00pm and 4.30pm during the Main Season. Mondays and Wednesdays are operated by a D.M.U.
Prices: Adult Return £5.00
Child Return £2.50
Family Ticket £14.00 (2 adult + 2 children)
Different fares may apply on special event days.

Detailed Directions by Car:
From All Parts: Embsay Station is off the A59 Skipton bypass by the Harrogate Road. Bolton Abbey Station is off the A59 at Bolton Abbey.

FAIRBOURNE & BARMOUTH RAILWAY

Address: Beach Road, Fairbourne, Dolgellau, Gwynedd LL38 2PZ
Telephone Nº: (01341) 250362
Year Formed: 1947
Location of Line: On A493 between Tywyn & Dolgellau
Length of Line: 2½ miles

Nº of Steam Locos: 4
Nº of Other Locos: 2
Nº of Members: 87
Annual Membership Fee: £8.00
Approx Nº of Visitors P.A.: 25,000
Gauge: 12¼ inches
Web Site: www.fairbourne-railway.co.uk

GENERAL INFORMATION

Nearest Railtrack Station: Fairbourne (adjacent)
Nearest Bus Station: Fairbourne (adjacent)
Car Parking: Free parking in Railtrack car park
Coach Parking: Pay & Display car park 300 yards (the Railway will re-imburse car parking charges for party bookings)
Souvenir Shop(s): Yes
Food & Drinks: Yes – Tea room at Fairbourne, Cafe at Porth Penrhyn Terminus

SPECIAL INFORMATION

There is a connecting ferry service (passenger only) to Barmouth from Porth Penrhyn Terminus.

OPERATING INFORMATION

Opening Times: Open daily from 1st May to September 22nd. Also opens from 28th March to 7th April and 26th October to 3rd November. Santa Specials run in December – phone for details.
Steam Working: 11.00am to 3.45pm for normal service. At peak times 10.40am to 4.20pm.
Prices: Adult £6.10
Child £3.75
Family £16.80 (2 adults + up to 3 children)
Senior Citizen £5.50

Detailed Directions by Car:
From North & East Wales: Follow Dolgellau signs, turn left onto A493 towards Tywyn. The turn-off for Fairbourne is located 9 miles south west of Dolgellau; From South Wales: Follow signs for Machynlleth, then follow A487 towards Dolgellau. Then take A493 towards Fairbourne.

FFESTINIOG RAILWAY

Address: Ffestiniog Railway, Harbour Station, Porthmadog, Gwynedd LL49 9NF	**N° of Steam Locos**: 12
	N° of Other Locos: 12
Telephone N°: (01766) 516073	**N° of Members**: 5,000
Year Formed: 1832	**Annual Membership Fee**: £18.00
Location of Line: Porthmadog to Blaenau Ffestiniog	**Approx N° of Visitors P.A.**: 200,000
	Gauge: 1 foot 11½ inches
Length of Line: 13½ miles	**Web Site**: www.festrail.co.uk

GENERAL INFORMATION

Nearest Railtrack Station: Blaenau Ffestiniog (interchange)
Nearest Bus Station: Bus stop next to stations at Porthmadog & Blaenau Ffestiniog
Car Parking: Parking available at Porthmadog, Blaenau Ffestiniog and Minffordd
Coach Parking: Available at Porthmadog and Blaenau Ffestiniog
Souvenir Shop(s): Yes
Food & Drinks: Yes

SPECIAL INFORMATION

The Railway runs through the spectacular scenery of Snowdonia National Park.

OPERATING INFORMATION

Opening Times: Daily service from the end of March to early November. Limited service in the Winter. Train times vary.
Steam Working: Most trains are steam hauled. Limited in the Winter, however.
Prices: Adult £14.00
Child £7.00 (1 child free with each adult)
Reductions are available for Senior Citizens and groups of 20 or more.

Detailed Directions by Car:
Portmadog is easily accessible from the Midlands – take the M54/A5 to Corwen then the A494 to Bala onto the A4212 to Trawsfynydd and the A470 (becomes the A487 from Maentwrog) to Porthmadog. From Chester take the A55 to Llandudno Junction and the A470 to Blaenau Ffestiniog. Both Stations are well-signposted.

FOXFIELD STEAM RAILWAY

Address: Caverswall Road Station, Blythe Bridge, Stoke-on-Trent, Staffs. ST11 9EA **Telephone Nº**: (01782) 396210 **Year Formed**: 1967 **Location of Line**: Blythe Bridge **Length of Line**: 3½ miles **Gauge**: Standard	**Nº of Steam Locos**: 16 **Nº of Other Locos**: 15 **Nº of Members**: Over 300 **Annual Membership Fee**: Adult £8.00; Junior £5.00; Family £12.00 **Approx Nº of Visitors P.A.**: 25,000

GENERAL INFORMATION

Nearest Railtrack Station: Blythe Bridge (¼ mile)
Nearest Bus Station: Hanley (5 miles)
Car Parking: Space for 300 cars available
Coach Parking: Space for 6 coaches available
Souvenir Shop(s): Yes
Food & Drinks: Yes – with a bar on the trains

SPECIAL INFORMATION

The Railway is a former Colliery railway built in 1893 to take coal from Foxfield Colliery. It has the steepest Standard Gauge adhesion worked gradient in the UK.

OPERATING INFORMATION

Opening Times: Sundays & Bank Holiday Mondays from 30th March to the end of September. Also weekends in December. Open 10.30am to 5.00pm.
Steam Working: 11.30am, 1.00pm, 2.00pm. 3.00pm & 4.00pm
Prices: Adult Tickets – £4.50
Child Tickets – £2.00
Senior Citizen Tickets – £3.50
Family Tickets – £12.00
Fares may vary on special event days.

Detailed Directions by Car:
From South: Exit M6 at Junction 14 onto the A34 to Stone then the A520 to Meir and the A50 to Blythe Bridge; From North: Exit M6 at Junction 15 then the A500 to Stoke-on-Trent and the A50 to Blythe Bridge; From East: Take the A50 to Blythe Bridge. Once in Blythe Bridge, turn by the Railtrack crossing.

GLOUCESTERSHIRE WARWICKSHIRE RAILWAY

Address: The Station, Toddington, Cheltenham, Gloucestershire GL54 5DT	**Nº of Steam Locos**: 11
Telephone Nº: (01242) 621405	**Nº of Other Locos**: 17
Year Formed: 1981	**Nº of Members**: 2,650
Location of Line: 5 miles south of	**Annual Membership Fee**: £11.00 (Adult)
Broadway, Worcestershire, near the A46	**Approx Nº of Visitors P.A.**: 50,000
Length of Line: 6½ miles	**Gauge**: Standard gauge
	Web site: www.gwsr.plc.uk

GENERAL INFORMATION

Nearest Railtrack Station: Cheltenham Spa or Ashchurch
Nearest Bus Station: Cheltenham
Car Parking: Parking available at Toddington and Winchcombe Stations
Coach Parking: Parking available as above
Souvenir Shop(s): Yes
Food & Drinks: Yes

SPECIAL INFORMATION

A narrow gauge railway is adjacent.

OPERATING INFORMATION

Opening Times: Sundays in November, January & February. Weekends & Bank Holidays during the rest of the year. Also daily during School Holidays. 10.00am to 5.00pm
Steam Working: Most operating days
Prices: Adult Return £7.00
Child Return £4.00
Senior Citizen Return £6.00
Family Return £19.00 (2 Adult + 2 Child)
Under 5's free of charge

Detailed Directions by Car:
Toddington is 11 miles north east of Cheltenham, 5 miles south of Broadway just off the B4632 (old A46). Exit the M5 at Junction 9 towards Stow-on-the-Wold for the B4632. The Railway is clearly visible from the B4632.

GREAT CENTRAL RAILWAY

Address: Great Central Station, Great Central Road, Loughborough, Leicestershire LE11 1RW **Telephone Nº**: (01509) 230726 **Year Formed**: 1969 **Location of Line**: From Loughborough to Leicester	**Length of Line**: 8 miles **Nº of Steam Locos**: 12 **Nº of Other Locos**: 6 **Nº of Members**: 5,000 **Annual Membership Fee**: £17.50 **Approx Nº of Visitors P.A.**: 150,000 **Gauge**: Standard

GENERAL INFORMATION

Nearest Railtrack Station: Loughborough (1 mile)
Nearest Bus Station: Loughborough (½ mile)
Car Parking: Street parking outside the Station
Coach Parking: Car parks at Quorn & Woodhouse, Rothley and Leicester North
Souvenir Shop(s): Yes
Food & Drinks: Yes – Buffet or Restaurant cars are usually available for snacks or other meals

SPECIAL INFORMATION

The aim of the GCR is to recreate the experience of British main line railway operation during the best years of steam locomotives.

OPERATING INFORMATION

Opening Times: Open daily throughout the year.
Steam Working: Weekends and Bank Holidays throughout the year. Also most weekdays from 28th May to 19th September and 21st to 25th October.
Prices: Adult Return £10.00
Child/Senior Citizen Return £6.70
Family Ticket £25.00 (2 adults + 3 children)

Detailed Directions by Car:
Great Central Road is on the South East side of Loughborough and is clearly signposted from the A6 Leicester Road and A60 Nottingham Road.

GROUDLE GLEN RAILWAY

Address: Groudle Glen, Onchan, Isle of Man	**N° of Steam Locos**: 2
	N° of Other Locos: 2
Telephone N°: (01624) 670453 (weekends)	**N° of Members**: 600
Year Formed: 1982 **Re-Opened**: 1986	**Annual Membership Fee**: £10.00
Location of Line: Groudle Glen	**Approx N° of Visitors P.A.**: 10,000
Length of Line: ¾ mile	**Correspondence**: 29 Hawarden Avenue,
Gauge: Narrow	Douglas, Isle of Man IM1 4BP

GENERAL INFORMATION

Nearest Railtrack Station: Manx Electric Railway
Nearest Bus Station: Douglas Bus Station
Car Parking: At the entrance to the Glen
Coach Parking: At the entrance to the Glen
Souvenir Shop(s): Yes
Food & Drinks: Coffee and Tea available

SPECIAL INFORMATION

The Railway runs through a picturesque glen to a coastal headland where there are the remains of a Victorian Zoo. The Railway was built in 1896 and closed in 1962.

OPERATING INFORMATION

Opening Times: Easter Sunday & Monday + Sundays from 5th May to 29th September 11.00am to 4.30pm. 30th June, 6th & 13th August + Wednesday evenings from 3th July to 14th August 7.00pm to 9.00pm. Santa trains run on 15th, 22nd and 26th December between 12.00pm and 3.30pm.
Steam Working: Phone the Railway for details.
Prices: Adult Return £2.00
           Child Return £1.00

Detailed Directions by Car:
The Railway is situated on the coast road to the north of Douglas.

GWILI RAILWAY

Address: Bronwydd Arms Station,
Bronwydd Arms, Carmarthen   SA33 6HT
Telephone Nº: (01267) 230666
Year Formed: 1975
Location of Line: Near Carmarthen,
South Wales
Length of Line: 2½ miles

Nº of Steam Locos: 5
Nº of Other Locos: 8
Nº of Members: 900 shareholders, 450
Society members
Annual Membership Fee: £10.00
Approx Nº of Visitors P.A.: 24,000
Gauge: Standard

GENERAL INFORMATION

Nearest Railtrack Station: Carmarthen (3 miles)
Nearest Bus Station: Carmarthen (3 miles)
Car Parking: Free parking at Bronwydd Arms
except for a few special occasions
Coach Parking: Free parking at Bronwydd Arms
Souvenir Shop(s): Yes
Food & Drinks: Yes

SPECIAL INFORMATION

Gwili Railway was the first Standard Gauge
preserved railway in Wales. There is a riverside picnic
area at Llwyfan Cerrig Station.
Web site: www.gwili-railway.co.uk

OPERATING INFORMATION

Opening Times: Daily from 27th July to 1st
September. Open over Easter, on Sundays in May,
June, July & September and Wednesdays in July. Also
open during school half-terms and dates in
December. Please phone for further details.
Steam Working: Most advertised trains are steam
hauled. Trains run from 11.15am to 4.30pm.
Prices: Adult £4.50
Child £3.00
Family £12.50 (2 adults + up to 3 children)
Senior Citizens £3.00

Detailed Directions by Car:
The Railway is three miles North of Carmarthen – signposted off the A484 Carmarthen to Cardigan Road.

HOLLYCOMBE STEAM COLLECTION

Address: Hollycombe, Liphook, Hants. GU30 7LP	**Nº of Steam Locos:** 3
Telephone Nº: (01428) 724900	**Nº of Other Locos:** 1
Year Formed: 1970	**Nº of Members:** 150
Location of Line: Hollycombe, Liphook	**Annual Membership Fee:** £8.00
Length of Line: 1¾ miles Narrow gauge, ¼ mile Standard gauge	**Approx Nº of Visitors P.A.:** 35,000
	Gauge: 2 feet (narrow gauge)
	Web site: www.hollycombe.co.uk

GENERAL INFORMATION

Nearest Railtrack Station: Liphook (1 mile)
Nearest Bus Station: Liphook
Car Parking: Extensive grass area
Coach Parking: Hardstanding for several
Souvenir Shop(s): Yes
Food & Drinks: Yes – Cafe

SPECIAL INFORMATION

The narrow gauge railway ascends to spectacular views of the Downs and is part of an extensive working steam museum.

OPERATING INFORMATION

Opening Times: Sundays & Bank Holidays from 29th March to 13th October. Open daily from 21st July to 26th August.
Steam Working: 1.00pm to 5.00pm
Prices: Adult £7.50
Child £6.00
Family £24.00 (4 people with no more than 2 adults)
Note: Prices are £1.00 less on Summer weekdays

Detailed Directions by Car:
Follow A3 to Liphook and follow the brown tourist signs.

ISLE OF MAN STEAM RAILWAY

Address: Isle of Man Transport, Banks Circus, Douglas, Isle of Man IM1 5PT	**Nº of Steam Locos**: 6
Telephone Nº: (01624) 663366	**Nº of Other Locos**: 1
Year Formed: 1873	**Nº of Members**: –
Location of Line: Douglas to Port Erin	**Annual Membership Fee**: –
Length of Line: 15½ miles	**Approx Nº of Visitors P.A.**: 100,000
	Gauge: 3 feet

GENERAL INFORMATION

Nearest Railtrack Station: Not applicable
Car Parking: Limited parking at all stations
Coach Parking: Available at Douglas & Port Erin
Souvenir Shop(s): None
Food & Drinks: Yes – Douglas & Port Erin stations

SPECIAL INFORMATION

The Isle of Man Steam Railway is operated by the Isle of Man Government. Due to track renewal works, the Railway will operate from Douglas to Santon and Castletown to Port Erin with coach connections during 2002.

OPERATING INFORMATION

Opening Times: Daily from 15th April to 27th October.
Steam Working: As above
Prices: Prices vary with 1, 3, 5 & 7 day Explorer tickets also available which include travel on buses and the Snaefell and Manx Electric Railways.

Detailed Directions:
By Sea from Heysham (Lancashire) or Liverpool to reach Isle of Man. Douglas Station is ½ mile inland from the Sea terminal and promenade (fully signposted).

ISLE OF WIGHT STEAM RAILWAY

Address: The Railway Station, Haven Street, Ryde, Isle of Wight PO33 4DS **Telephone Nº:** (01983) 882204 **Year Formed:** 1971 (re-opened) **Location:** Smallbrook Junction to Wootton **Length of Line:** 5 miles **Nº of Steam Locos:** 6	**Nº of Other Locos:** 3 **Nº of Members:** 1,300 **Annual Membership Fee:** £15.00 **Approx Nº of Visitors P.A.:** 100,000 **Gauge:** Standard **Talking Timetable:** (01983) 884343 **Web site:** www.iwsteamrailway.co.uk

GENERAL INFORMATION

Nearest Railtrack Station: Smallbrook Junction (direct interchange)
Nearest Bus: From Ryde & Newport direct
Car Parking: Free parking at Havenstreet & Wootton Stations
Coach Parking: Free at Havenstreet Station
Souvenir Shop(s): Yes – at Havenstreet Station
Food & Drinks: Yes – at Havenstreet Station

SPECIAL INFORMATION

The IWSR uses mostly Victorian & Edwardian locomotives and carriages to recreate the atmosphere of an Isle of Wight branch line railway.

OPERATING INFORMATION

Opening Times: Selected days between March and October and daily from 1st June to 29th September
Steam Working: 10.30am to 4.00pm (depending on the Station)
Prices: Adult Return £7.50
Child Return £4.00
Family Return £19.00
(2 adults + 2 children)

Detailed Directions by Car:
To reach the Isle of Wight head for the Ferry ports at Lymington, Southampton or Portsmouth. From all parts of the Isle of Wight, head for Ryde and follow the brown tourist signs.

KEIGHLEY & WORTH VALLEY RAILWAY

Address: The Station, Haworth, Keighley, West Yorkshire BD22 8NJ
Telephone Nº: (01535) 645214 (enquiries); (01535) 647777 (24 hour timetable)
Year Formed: 1962 (Line re-opened 1968)
Location of Line: From Keighley southwards through Haworth to Oxenhope
Length of Line: 4¾ miles

Nº of Steam Locos: 30
Nº of Other Locos: 10
Members: 4,500 (350 working members)
Annual Membership Fee: Adult £14.00; Adult life membership £250.00
Approx Nº of Visitors P.A.: 150,000
Gauge: Standard
Web Site: http://www.kwvr.co.uk

GENERAL INFORMATION

Nearest Railtrack Station: Keighley (adjacent)
Nearest Bus Station: Keighley (5 minutes walk)
Car Parking: Parking at Keighley, Ingrow, Haworth (charged) and Oxenhope
Coach Parking: At Ingrow & Oxenhope (phone in advance)
Souvenir Shop(s): Yes – at Keighley, Haworth & Oxenhope
Food & Drinks: Yes – at Keighley & Oxenhope when trains run.

OPERATING INFORMATION

Opening Times: Weekends & Bank Holidays throughout the year. Daily from 9th July to 2nd September. Also open during Easter, Whit, October School holidays and 26th December to 1st January.
Steam Working: Early trains are Diesel; Steam runs from mid-morning on all operating days (except 4 weekends prior to Christmas).
Prices: Adult Return £6.00; £8.00 day rover
Child Return £3.00; £4.00 day rover
Family Return £16.00 (2 adults, 3 children)
Family Day Rover £20.00

Detailed Directions by Car:
Exit the M62 at Junction 26 and take the M606 to its' end. Follow the ring-road signs around Bradford to Shipley. Take the A650 through Bingley to Keighley and follow the brown tourist signs to the railway. Alternatively, take the A6033 from Hebden Bridge to Oxenhope and follow the brown signs to Oxenhope or Haworth Stations.

Kent & East Sussex Railway

Address: Tenterden Town Station, Tenterden, Kent TN30 6HE	**N° of Steam Locos**: 12
	N° of Other Locos: 6
Telephone N°: (01580) 765155	**N° of Members**: 3,000
Year Formed: 1973	**Annual Membership Fee**: £20.00
Location of Line: Tenterden, Kent to Bodiam, East Sussex	**Approx N° of Visitors P.A.**: 110,000
	Gauge: Standard
Length of Line: 10½ miles	**Web site**: www.kesr.org.uk

GENERAL INFORMATION

Nearest Railtrack Station: Headcorn (10 miles)
Nearest Bus Station: Tenterden
Car Parking: Parking at Tenterden Town & Northiam Stations
Coach Parking: As above
Souvenir Shop(s): Yes
Food & Drinks: Yes

SPECIAL INFORMATION

Built as Britain's first light railway, the K&ESR opened in 1900 and was epitomised by sharp curved and steep gradients and to this day retains a charm and atmosphere all of its own.

OPERATING INFORMATION

Opening Times: Daily from March to October and in December. The return journey time is 1 hour 55 minutes.
Steam Working: Every operational day
Prices: Adult Ticket − £8.00
Child Ticket − £4.00
Family Ticket − £23.00

Detailed Directions by Car:
From London and Kent Coast: Travel to Ashford (M20) then take the A28 to Tenterden; From Sussex Coast: Take A28 from Hastings to Northiam.

KIRKLEES LIGHT RAILWAY

Address: Park Mill Way, Clayton West, near Huddersfield, W. Yorks. HD8 9XJ
Telephone Nº: (01484) 865727
Year Formed: 1991
Location of Line: Clayton West to Shelley
Length of Line: 4 miles

Nº of Steam Locos: 4
Nº of Other Locos: 2
Nº of Members: –
Annual Membership Fee: –
Approx Nº of Visitors P.A.: –
Gauge: 15 inches

GENERAL INFORMATION

Nearest Railtrack Station: Denby Dale (4 miles)
Nearest Bus Station: Bus stop outside gates. Take 484 from Wakefield or 235 from Huddersfield/Barnsley.
Car Parking: Ample free parking at site
Coach Parking: Ample free parking at site
Souvenir Shop(s): Yes
Food & Drinks: Yes

SPECIAL INFORMATION

A new station and visitor centre opened in 1998.

OPERATING INFORMATION

Opening Times: Open every weekend and most school holidays in the Winter. Open daily from 27th May to 1st September.
Steam Working: All trains are steam-hauled. Trains run hourly from 11.00am
Prices: Adults £5.00
Children (3-15 years) £3.50
Children (under 3 years) Free of charge

Detailed Directions by Car:
The Railway is located on the A636 Wakefield to Denby Dale road. Turn off the M1 at Junction 38 and the railway is 4 miles on the left after going under the railway bridge, just before the village of Scissett.

LAKESIDE & HAVERTHWAITE RAILWAY

Address: Haverthwaite Station, near Ulverston, Cumbria   LA12 8AL
Telephone N°: (015395) 31594
Year Formed: 1973
Location of Line: Haverthwaite to Lakeside
Length of Line: 3½ miles

N° of Steam Locos: 8
N° of Other Locos: 6
N° of Members: 250
Annual Membership Fee: £10.00 Adult, £5.00 Juniors
Approx N° of Visitors P.A.: 170,000
Gauge: Standard

GENERAL INFORMATION

Nearest Railtrack Station: Ulverston (7 miles)
Nearest Bus Station: Haverthwaite (100 yards)
Car Parking: Plenty of spaces – £1.00 charge
Coach Parking: Free parking at site
Souvenir Shop(s): Yes
Food & Drinks: Yes

SPECIAL INFORMATION

Connections are available at Lakeside for Windermere Lake Cruises to Bowness & Ambleside. Through tickets are available.

OPERATING INFORMATION

Opening Times: Daily from 23rd March to 7th April. Weekends in April then daily from 4th May to 27th October. Santa Specials run on 7th, 8th, 14th, 15th, 21st & 22nd of December.
Steam Working: Daily from morning to late afternoon.
Prices: Adult Return £4.10; Single £2.40
Child Return £2.05; Single £1.65
Family Ticket £11.60

Detailed Directions by Car:
From All Parts: Exit the M6 at Junction 36 and follow the brown tourist signs.

Lappa Valley Steam Railway

Address: St. Newlyn East, Newquay, Cornwall TR8 5HZ
Telephone N°: (01872) 510317
Year Formed: 1974
Location of Line: Benny Halt to East Wheal Rose, near St. Newlyn East
Length of Line: 1 mile

N° of Steam Locos: 2
N° of Other Locos: 2
N° of Members: –
Annual Membership Fee: –
Approx N° of Visitors P.A.: 50,000
Gauge: 15 inches
Web site: www.lappavalley.co.uk

GENERAL INFORMATION

Nearest Railtrack Station: Newquay (5 miles)
Nearest Bus Station: Newquay (5 miles)
Car Parking: Free parking at Benny Halt
Coach Parking: Free parking at Benny Halt
Souvenir Shop(s): Yes
Food & Drinks: Yes

SPECIAL INFORMATION

The railway runs on part of the former Newquay to Chacewater branch line. Site also has a Grade II listed mine building, boating, play areas for children and 2 other miniature train rides.

OPERATING INFORMATION

Opening Times: Easter to October (daily from Easter to September inclusive). Limited opening during October – please phone the Railway for further details.
Steam Working: 10.30am to 4.30pm or later on operating days
Prices: Adult £6.00
Child £4.00
Family £17.50 (2 adults + 2 children)

Detailed Directions by Car:
The railway is signposted from the A30 at the Summercourt-Mitchell bypass, from the A3075 south of Newquay and the A3058 east of Newquay.

LAUNCESTON STEAM RAILWAY

Address: The Old Gasworks, St. Thomas' Road, Launceston, Cornwall   PL15 8DA
Telephone Nº: (01566) 775665
Year Formed: Opened in 1983
Location of Line: Launceston to Newmills
Length of Line: 2½ miles

Nº of Steam Locos: 5 (3 working)
Nº of Other Locos: 2 Diesel, 1 Electric
Nº of Members: –
Annual Membership Fee: –
Gauge: 1 foot 11 ⅝ inches

GENERAL INFORMATION

Nearest Railtrack Station: Liskeard (15 miles)
Nearest Bus Station: Launceston (½ mile) – Devon Bus services stop at the Railway on Sundays only
Car Parking: At Station, Newport Industrial Estate, Launceston
Coach Parking: As above
Souvenir Shop(s): Yes – also with a bookshop
Food & Drinks: Yes – Cafe, snacks & drinks

SPECIAL INFORMATION

During the Summer school holidays, two engines are sometimes in operation. On Sundays, Dartmoor and Tamar Valley 'Rover Tickets' are available.

OPERATING INFORMATION

Opening Times: Good Friday for 8 days then Spring Bank Holiday for 6 days. Open from Sundays to Wednesdays in June and Sundays to Fridays from July to September. Also during half-term in October.
Steam Working: 11.00am to 4.30pm on operational days
Prices: Adult £5.50 (may increase)
  Child £3.70 (may increase)
  Family £18.00 (2 adults + 4 children)
  Senior Citizen £5.00
Group rates are available upon application. These prices include as many trips as you like on the day of purchase.

Detailed Directions by Car:
Drive to Launceston and look for the brown Steam Engine Tourist signs. Use the L.S.R. car park at the Newport Industrial Estate.

THE LAVENDER LINE

Address: Isfield Station, Isfield, near Uckfield, East Sussex   TN22 5XB
Telephone Nº: (01825) 750515
Year Formed: 1992
Location of Line: East Sussex between Lewes and Uckfield
Length of Line: ¾ mile

Nº of Steam Locos: 2
Nº of Other Locos: 16
Nº of Members: Approximately 400
Annual Membership Fee: £10.00
Approx Nº of Visitors P.A.: 12,500
Gauge: Standard
Web site: www.lavender-line.co.uk

GENERAL INFORMATION

Nearest Railtrack Station: Uckfield (3 miles)
Nearest Bus Station: Uckfield (3 miles)
Car Parking: Free parking at site
Coach Parking: Can cater for coach parties – please contact the Railway.
Souvenir Shop: Yes
Food & Drinks: Yes – Cinders Buffet

SPECIAL INFORMATION

Isfield Station has been restored as a Southern Railway country station complete with the original L.B.S.C.R. signalbox.
Information Line: (09068) 800645

OPERATING INFORMATION

Opening Times: Sundays throughout the year. Saturdays and Sundays in June, July and August plus Wednesdays and Thursdays in August. Also open on Bank Holidays and in December for Santa Specials.
Steam Working: Please phone for details.
Prices: Adult £4.50
Child £2.50
Senior Citizen £3.50
Family (2 adults + 2 children) £11.50
All tickets offer unlimited rides on the day of issue and prices may vary on special event days.

Detailed Directions by Car::
From All Parts: Isfield is just off the A26 midway between Lewes and Uckfield.

LEIGHTON BUZZARD RAILWAY

Address: Pages Park Station, Billington Road, Leighton Buzzard, Beds. LU7 4TN	**Nº of Steam Locos**: 12
Telephone Nº: (01525) 373888	**Nº of Other Locos**: 41
Year Formed: 1967	**Nº of Members**: 340
Location of Line: Leighton Buzzard	**Annual Membership Fee**: £13.00
Length of Line: 3 miles	**Approx Nº of Visitors P.A.**: 20,000
	Gauge: 2 feet

GENERAL INFORMATION

Nearest Railtrack Station: Leighton Buzzard (2 miles)
Nearest Bus Station: Leighton Buzzard (¾ mile)
Car Parking: Free parking adjacent
Coach Parking: Free parking adjacent
Souvenir Shop(s): Yes
Food & Drinks: Yes

Web site: www.buzzrail.co.uk

OPERATING INFORMATION

Opening Times: Sundays from mid-March to late-October and also December. Open on bank holidays and in August (except for Mondays and Fridays). Also open on some Saturdays and Wednesdays throughout the year. Trains run from mid-morning to late afternoon.
Steam Working: Most operating days.
Prices: Adult £5.00
　　　　　Child £2.00
　　　　　Senior Citizens £4.00

Detailed Directions by Car:
The railway is 15 minutes drive from Junctions 11-13 of the M1. Follow the brown tourist signs in Leighton Buzzard or from the A505. Pages Park Station is ¾ mile from the Town Centre on the A4146 Hemel Hempstead road.

LINCOLNSHIRE WOLDS RAILWAY

Address: The Railway Station, Ludborough, Lincolnshire   DN36 5SQ
Telephone Nº: (01507) 363881
Year Formed: 1979
Location of Line: Ludborough – off the A16(T) between Grimsby and Louth
Length of Line: ¾ mile

Nº of Steam Locos: 4
Nº of Other Locos: 7
Nº of Members: Approximately 400+
Annual Membership Fee: £14.00 Family, £7.00 Adult, £4.50 Senior Citizen or Child
Approx Nº of Visitors P.A.: 3,200
Gauge: Standard

GENERAL INFORMATION

Nearest Railtrack Station: Grimsby (8 miles)
Nearest Bus Stop: Ludborough (½ mile)
Car Parking: 100 spaces for cars at the Station
Coach Parking: Space for 1 coach only
Souvenir Shop(s): Yes
Food & Drinks: Yes

SPECIAL INFORMATION

The buildings and facilities at Ludborough have been completed and short steam trips commenced in 1998. Plans to extend the line to North Thoresby (1 mile) are being pursued.

OPERATING INFORMATION

Opening Times: 21/28 April; 5/26 May; 2/3 June; 7/8 July; 11/25 August; 14/15 September; 8/15 December.
Steam Working: 11.00am to 4.00pm from April to October. 11.00am to 3.00pm November to March.
Prices: Adults £2.00
          Senior Citizens/Children £1.00
          Family £5.00 (2 adults + 4 children)
Different fares may apply at Special Events.
Day tickets are available on request.

Detailed Directions by Car:
The Railway is situated near Ludborough, ½ mile off the A16(T) Louth to Grimsby road. Follow signs to Fulstow to reach the station (approximately ½ mile). Do not turn into Ludborough but stay on the bypass.

LLANBERIS LAKE RAILWAY

Address: Gilfach Ddu, Llanberis, Gwynedd LL55 4TY
Telephone Nº: (01286) 870549
Year Formed: 1970
Location of Line: Just off the A4086 Caernarfon to Capel Curig road at Llanberis
Length of Line: 2 miles

Nº of Steam Locos: 3
Nº of Other Locos: 4
Nº of Members: −
Annual Membership Fee: −
Approx Nº of Visitors P.A.: 70,000
Gauge: 1 foot 11½ inches

GENERAL INFORMATION

Nearest Railtrack Station: Bangor (8 miles)
Nearest Bus Station: Caernarfon (6 miles)
Car Parking: £1.50 Council car park on site
Coach Parking: Ample free parking on site
Souvenir Shop(s): Yes
Food & Drinks: Yes

SPECIAL INFORMATION

Llanberis Lake Railway runs along part of the trackbed of the Padarn Railway which transported slates for export and closed in 1961.
Web Site: http://www.lake-railway.co.uk

OPERATING INFORMATION

Opening Times: Open most days from 11th March to 31st October. Please send for a free timetable.
Steam Working: 11.30am to 4.30pm on most days.
Prices: Adult £4.50
　　　　　Child £3.00
Various Family ticket options are available.
N.B. The Welsh Slate Museum is adjacent to the Railway.

Detailed Directions by Car:
The railway is situated just off the A4086 Caernarfon to Capel Curig road. Follow signs for Padarn Country Park.

LLANGOLLEN RAILWAY

Address: The Station, Abbey Road, Llangollen, Denbighshire LL20 8SN
Telephone Nº: (01978) 860979
Year Formed: 1975
Location of Line: Valley of the River Dee from Llangollen to Carrog
Length of Line: 7½ miles

Nº of Steam Locos: 14
Nº of Other Locos: 10
Nº of Members: 1,300
Annual Membership Fee: Adult £13.00; Family £20.00; Junior (under-16) £8.00
Approx Nº of Visitors P.A.: 90,000
Gauge: Standard

GENERAL INFORMATION

Nearest Railtrack Station: Ruabon (6 miles)
Nearest Bus Station: Wrexham (12 miles)
Car Parking: Public car park at Lower Dee Mill off A539 Ruabon road.
Coach Parking: Market Street car park in town centre
Souvenir Shop(s): Yes – at Llangollen Station
Food & Drinks: Yes – at Llangollen, Berwyn, Glyndyfrdwy and Carrog Stations.

SPECIAL INFORMATION

The route originally formed part of the line from Ruabon to Barmouth Junction, closed in 1964. The railway has been rebuilt by volunteers over the past 21 years, reopening to Carrog in 1996. The ultimate aim is to reopen to Corwen (10 miles).

OPERATING INFORMATION

Opening Times: Services in April and May then daily from June to October. Open weekends throughout the year. Opens from 10.00am to 6.00pm
Steam Working: Phone the Talking timetable number for further details: (01978) 860951
Prices: Adult Return £8.00 (Llangollen to Carrog)
Child Return £3.80
Family £18.00 (2 adults + 3 children)
Senior Citizens £5.50
Web Site: www.llangollen-railway.co.uk

Detailed Directions by Car:
From South & West: Go via the A5 to Llangollen. At the traffic lights turn into Castle Street to the River bridge; From North & East: Take the A483 to A539 junction and then via Trefor to Llangollen River bridge. The Station is adjacent to the River Dee.

Mangapps Railway Museum

Address: Southminster Road, Burnham-on-Crouch, Essex CM0 8QQ	**Nº of Steam Locos**: 5
Telephone Nº: (01621) 784898	**Nº of Other Locos**: 5
Year Formed: 1989	**Nº of Members**: –
Location of Line: Mangapps Farm	**Annual Membership Fee**: –
Length of Line: ¾ mile	**Approx Nº of Visitors P.A.**: 20,000
	Gauge: Standard

GENERAL INFORMATION

Nearest Railtrack Station: Burnham-on-Crouch (1 mile)
Nearest Bus Station: –
Car Parking: Ample free parking at site
Coach Parking: Ample free parking at site
Souvenir Shop(s): Yes
Food & Drinks: Yes – drinks and snacks only

SPECIAL INFORMATION

The Railway endeavours to recreate the atmosphere of an East Anglian light railway. It also includes an extensive museum with an emphasis on East Anglian items and signalling.

Web Site: www.mangapps.co.uk

OPERATING INFORMATION

Opening Times: Closed during January, then open every weekend and bank holiday (except over Christmas). Open every day during the Easter Fortnight and August. Special events in 2002: 'Day Out With Thomas' March 9th/10th/16th/17th. April 27th/28th. May 4th/5th/6th. July 6th/7th/13th/14th and October 19th/20th/26th/27th. Santa Specials run during weekends in December.
Steam Working: 1st Sunday of the month, every Sunday during August and December plus bank holidays. Diesel at other times.
Prices: Adult – Steam £5.00; Diesel £4.00
            Child – Steam £2.50; Diesel £2.00
N.B. Prices for special events may differ.

Detailed Directions by Car:
From South & West: From M25 take either the A12 or A127 and then the A130 to Rettendon Turnpike and then follow signs to Burnham; From North: From A12 take A414 to Oak Corner then follow signs to Burnham.

THE MIDDLETON RAILWAY

Address: The Station, Moor Road, Hunslet, Leeds   LS10 2JQ
Telephone N°: (0113) 271-0320
Year Formed: 1960
Location of Line: Moor Road to Middleton Park
Length of Line: 1½ miles

N° of Steam Locos: 15
N° of Other Locos: 12
Annual Membership Fee: Adults £9.50
Approx N° of Visitors P.A.: 20,000
Gauge: Standard
Web Site: www.middletonrailway.org.uk

GENERAL INFORMATION

Nearest Railtrack Station: Leeds City (1 mile)
Nearest Bus Station: Leeds (1½ miles)
Car Parking: Free parking at site
Coach Parking: Free parking at site
Souvenir Shop(s): Yes
Food & Drinks: Yes

SPECIAL INFORMATION

The Middleton Railway is the world's oldest working railway, founded in 1758. Passenger services run from the station into Middleton Park. A large collection of preserved industrial steam and diesel engines are displayed, many of them more than 100 years old.

OPERATING INFORMATION

Opening Times: Weekends & Bank Holidays from late March to December. Open 10.30am to 5.00pm
Steam Working: 11.00am to 4.20pm on Sundays and Bank Holidays.
Prices: Adult £2.50
Child £1.50
Family £7.00 (2 adults + 2 children)
Tickets provide for unlimited travel on the day of issue.
Please send SAE for the timetable and details of special events.

Detailed Directions by Car:
From the M1 Northbound: Take the M621 from Leeds City Centre and exit at Junction 5, turn right at the top of the slip road and take 3rd exit at the roundabout. The entrance to the Railway is 50 yards on the right. The railway is also signposted from the A61 and A653.

MID-HANTS RAILWAY (WATERCRESS LINE)

Address: The Railway Station, Alresford, Hampshire SO24 9JG
Telephone Nº: (01962) 733810 General enquiries; (01962) 734866 Timetable
Year Formed: 1977
Location of Line: Alresford to Alton
Length of Line: 10 miles

Nº of Steam Locos: 17
Nº of Other Locos: 8
Nº of Members: 4,500
Annual Membership Fee: Adult £17.50
Approx Nº of Visitors P.A.: 130,000
Gauge: Standard
Web Site: www.watercressline.co.uk

GENERAL INFO

Nearest Railtrack Station: Alton (adjacent) or Winchester (7 miles)
Nearest Bus Station: Winchester
Car Parking: Pay and display at Alton and Alresford Stations (Alresford free on Sundays & Bank Holidays)
Coach Parking: By arrangement at Alresford Station
Souvenir Shop(s): At Alresford, Ropley & Alton
Food & Drinks: Yes – Buffet on most trains. 'West Country' buffet at Alresford

SPECIAL INFO

The railway runs through four fully restored stations and has a Loco yard and picnic area at Ropley.

OPERATING INFO

Opening Times: Weekends and Bank Holidays from February to October. Weekdays from May to September and during School Holidays. Weekends and other dates in December.
Steam Working: All operating days.
Prices: Adult £9.00
Child (age 3 to 16) £2.00
Senior Citizens £8.00
Family £20.00
(2 adults + 2 children)
A 15% discount off these prices is available for pre-booked parties of 15 or more people. Write or call for a booking form.

Detailed Directions by Car:
From the East: Take the M25 then A3 and A31 to Alton; From the West: Exit the M3 at Junction 9 and take the A31 to Alresford Station.

MIDLAND RAILWAY CENTRE

Address: Butterley Station, Ripley, Derbyshire DE5 3QZ	**Nº of Steam Locos**: 25
Telephone Nº: (01773) 747674	**Nº of Other Locos**: 53
Year Formed: 1969	**Nº of Members**: 2,000
Location of Line: Butterley, near Ripley	**Annual Membership Fee**: £12.00
Length of Line: Standard gauge 3½ miles, Narrow gauge 0.8 mile	**Approx Nº of Visitors P.A.**: 130,000
	Gauge: Standard and various Narrow gauges including miniature

GENERAL INFORMATION

Nearest Railtrack Station: Alfreton (6 miles)
Nearest Bus Station: Bus stop outside Butterley Station.
Car Parking: Free parking at site – ample space
Coach Parking: Free parking at site
Souvenir Shop(s): Yes – at Butterley and Swanwick
Food & Drinks: Yes – both sites + bar on train

SPECIAL INFORMATION

The Centre is a unique project with a huge Museum development together with narrow gauge, miniature & model railways as well as a country park and farm park. Includes an Award-winning Victorian Railwaymans church and Princess Royal Class Locomotive Trust Depot.

OPERATING INFORMATION

Opening Times: The centre is open daily – trains do not run every day it is open however.
Steam Working: Weekends and bank holidays throughout the year. Wednesdays April to October and most days in the school holidays. Phone for further details. 'Day Out With Thomas' 2002 events: 2nd & 3rd March, 1st-9th June, 3rd-11th August.
Prices: Adult £7.95   Senior Citizens £6.50
Two children travel free with each paying adult.

Detailed Directions by Car:
From All Parts: From the M1 exit at Junction 28 and take the A38 towards Derby. The Centre is signposted at the junction with the B6179.

MOORS VALLEY RAILWAY

Address: Moors Valley Country Park, Horton Road, Ashley Heath, Nr. Ringwood, Hants. BH24 2ET	**Length of Line:** 1 mile
	N° of Steam Locos: 13
	N° of Other Locos: 1
Telephone N°: (01425) 471415	**N° of Members:** –
Year Formed: 1985	**Approx N° of Visitors P.A.:** –
Location of Line: Moors Valley Country Park	**Gauge:** 7¼ inches
	Web site: www.moorsvalleyrailway.co.uk

GENERAL INFORMATION

Nearest Railtrack Station: Bournemouth (12 miles)
Nearest Bus Station: Ringwood (3 miles)
Car Parking: Parking charge varies throughout the year. Maximum charge £5.00 per day.
Coach Parking: Charges are applied for parking
Souvenir Shop(s): Yes + Model Railway Shop
Food & Drinks: Yes

SPECIAL INFORMATION

The Moors Valley Railway is a complete small Railway with signalling and 2 signal boxes and also 4 tunnels and 2 level crossings.

OPERATING INFORMATION

Opening Times: Weekends throughout the year. Daily from one week before to one week after Easter, Spring Bank Holiday to mid-September, during School half-term holidays and also from Boxing Day to end of School holidays. Also Santa Specials in December and occasional other openings. Phone the Railways for details.
Steam Working: 10.45am to 5.00pm when open.
Prices: Adult Return £2.30; Adult Single £1.25
Child Return £1.55; Child Single 85p
Special rates are available for parties of 10 or more.

Detailed Directions by Car:
From All Parts: Moors Valley Country Park is situated on Horton Road which is off the A31 Ferndown to Ringwood road near the junction with the A338 to Bournemouth.

MULL & WEST HIGHLAND RAILWAY

Address: Old Pier Station, Craignure, Isle of Mull, Argyll PA65 6AY **Telephone Nº**: (01680) 812494 **Web Site**: www.holidaymull.org/rail/Welcome **Year Formed**: 1983 **Location of Line**: Isle of Mull **Length of Line**: 1¼ miles	**Gauge**: 10¼ inches **Nº of Steam Locos**: 3 **Nº of Other Locos**: 3 **Nº of Members**: 30 (also Friends of the Railway) **Annual Membership Fee**: £5.00 **Approx Nº of Visitors P.A.**: 30,000

GENERAL INFORMATION

Nearest Railtrack Station: Oban (11 miles by Cal-Mac Ferry)
Nearest Bus Station: Oban (as above)
Car Parking: Free parking on site at Craignure
Coach Parking: Free parking at site
Souvenir Shop(s): Yes
Food & Drinks: No – but drinks & sweets available

SPECIAL INFORMATION

This narrow gauge railway was the first passenger railway to be built on a Scottish island. It was built specially to link Torosay Castle & Gardens to the main Port of entry at Craignure.

OPERATING INFORMATION

Opening Times: Daily from 28th March to 19th October. Opens 11.00am to 5.00pm.
Steam Working: Steam and diesel trains are run depending on operational requirements.
Prices: Adult Single £2.50; Adult Return £3.50
             Child Single £1.50; Child Return £2.50
             Family Tickets (2 adults + 2 children)
             Single £6.00; Return £9.50
Joint Sail/Rail tickets available from Cal-Mac in Oban.

Detailed Directions by Car:
Once off the ferry, turn left at the end of the pier, go straight on for almost ½ mile then turn left at the thistle sign opposite the Police station and carry straight on until you reach the station car park.

NENE VALLEY RAILWAY

Address: Wansford Station, Stibbington, Peterborough PE8 6LR	**Nº of Steam Locos**: 17
Telephone Nº: (01780) 784444 enquiries; (01780) 784404 talking timetable	**Nº of Other Locos**: 11
	Nº of Members: 1,300
Year Formed: 1977	**Annual Membership Fee**: Adult £11.50; Child £6.50; Joint £18.50; OAP £6.50
Location: Off A1 to west of Peterborough	**Approx Nº of Visitors P.A.**: 65,000
Length of Line: 7½ miles	**Gauge**: Standard

GENERAL INFORMATION

Nearest Railtrack Station: Peterborough (¾ mile)
Nearest Bus Station: Peterborough (Queensgate – ¾ mile)
Car Parking: Free parking at Wansford & Orton Mere
Coach Parking: Free coach parking at Wansford
Souvenir Shop(s): Yes
Food & Drinks: Yes

SPECIAL INFORMATION

The railway is truly international in flavour with British and Continental locomotives and rolling stock.

Web site: www.nvr.org.uk

OPERATING INFORMATION

Opening Times: Sundays from January to the end of October. Saturdays from Easter to end of October. Mid-week on various dates from May to the end of August and also at various other times. Contact the Railway for complete details. Open 9.00am to 4.30pm.
Steam Working: Most services are steam hauled apart from on diesel days and times of high fire risk.
Prices: Adult £10.00
     Child £4.00 (ages 3 to 15)
     Family £20.00 (2 adults + 3 children)
     Senior Citizens/Disabled £6.00

Detailed Directions by Car:
The railway is situated off the southbound carriageway of the A1 between the A47 and A605 junctions – west of Peterborough and south of Stamford.

NORTHAMPTON & LAMPORT RAILWAY

Address: Pitsford & Bramford Station, Pitsford Road, Chapel Brampton, Northampton   NN6 8BA
Telephone Nº: (01604) 820327 (infoline)
Year Formed: 1983 (became operational in November 1995)
Web site: www.nlr.org.uk

Length of Line: 1 mile at present
Nº of Steam Locos: 5
Nº of Other Locos: 8
Nº of Members: 650
Annual Membership Fee: £10.00
Approx Nº of Visitors P.A.: 24,000
Gauge: Standard

GENERAL INFORMATION

Nearest Railtrack Station: Northampton (5 miles)
Nearest Bus Station: Northampton (5 miles)
Car Parking: Free parking at site
Coach Parking: Free parking at site
Souvenir Shop(s): Yes
Food & Drinks: Yes

SPECIAL INFORMATION

A developing railway – this became operational again on 18th November 1995.

OPERATING INFORMATION

Opening Times: Sundays and Bank holidays from March to October. Santa Specials in December. Open 10.30am to 5.00pm. 'Day out with Thomas' dates: 4/5/6 May; 24/25/26 August; 9/10 November
Steam Working: Generally between April and September and also in December.
Prices: Adult £3.20
            Child £2.10
            Family £8.50 (2 adults + 2 children)
Fares may vary on Special Event days.

Detailed Directions by Car:
The station is situated along the Pitsford road at Chapel Brampton, approximately 5 miles north of Northampton. Heading north out of town, it is signposted to the right on the A5199 (A50) Welford Road at Chapel Brampton crossroads or on the left on the A508 Market Harborough road at the Pitsford turn.

NORTH NORFOLK RAILWAY

Address: Sheringham Station, Sheringham, Norfolk NR26 8RA	**Nº of Steam Locos**: 4
Telephone Nº: (01263) 820800	**Nº of Other Locos**: 5
Year Formed: 1975	**Nº of Members**: 1,000
Location of Line: Sheringham to Holt via Weybourne	**Annual Membership Fee**: £12.00
Length of Line: 5¼ miles	**Approx Nº of Visitors P.A.**: 100,000
	Gauge: Standard
	Web site: www.nnr.co.uk

GENERAL INFORMATION

Nearest Railtrack Station: Sheringham (200 yards)
Nearest Bus Station: Outside the Station
Car Parking: Adjacent to all three stations
Coach Parking: Adjacent to all three stations
Souvenir Shop(s): Yes – at all three stations
Food & Drinks: Yes – main catering facilities at Sheringham Station

SPECIAL INFORMATION

Sheringham Station has a museum coach and signalbox. The railway is the only full-sized preserved Steam railway in Norfolk.

OPERATING INFORMATION

Opening Times: Most days from 23rd March to 27th October plus weekends in November and December.
Steam Working: 11.00am to 5.00pm
Prices: Adult £7.50
   Child £4.00   (Under 4's free of charge)
   Family £21.00
   Senior Citizens £6.50
All the above prices are all-day tickets.
Special events: Golden Jubilee – 1st to 9th June;
Steam Gala – 6th to 8th September;
1940's Weekend – 21st and 22nd September.

Detailed Directions by Car:
The railway is situated on the A149 Cromer to Sheringham road. All 3 stations are signposted from this road.

NORTH YORKSHIRE MOORS RAILWAY

Address: Pickering Station, Pickering, North Yorkshire YO18 7AJ	**Length of Line**: 18 miles
Telephone Nº: (01751) 472508 (enquiries)	**Nº of Steam Locos**: 20
	Nº of Other Locos: 12
Web site: www.northyorkshiremoorsrailway.com	**Nº of Members**: 8,000
Year Formed: 1967	**Annual Membership Fee**: Adult £14.00; Over 60's £10.00
Location of Line: Pickering to Grosmont via stations at Levisham and Goathland	**Approx Nº of Visitors P.A.**: 280,000
	Gauge: Standard

GENERAL INFORMATION

Nearest Railtrack Station: Grosmont (opposite NYMR station)
Nearest Bus Station: Pickering (½ mile)
Car Parking: Available at each station
Coach Parking: Available at Pickering & Grosmont
Souvenir Shop(s): Yes – at Pickering, Goathland and Grosmont
Food & Drinks: Pickering, Grosmont & Goathland

SPECIAL INFORMATION

The NYMR runs through the spectacular North Yorks Moors and is the most popular in the country. As seen in 'Heartbeat' and also used in the filming of 'Harry Potter and the Philosopher's Stone'.

OPERATING INFORMATION

Opening Times: Open daily from 23rd March to 3rd November.
Steam Working: Usually daily – please phone the Railway for timetable information
Prices: Adult £10.00 (all-day travel)
  Child £5.00 (all-day travel)
Family Tickets start at £23.00 for 2 adults & 1 child –
  £25.00 for 2 adults and 2 children
  £27.00 for 2 adults and 3 children
  £29.00 for 2 adults and 4 children

Detailed Directions by Car:
From the South: Follow signs to York, follow the A64 to Malton then take the A169 from Malton to Pickering; From the North: Take A171 to Whitby and then the A169 to Grosmont.

NOTTINGHAM TRANSPORT HERITAGE CENTRE

Address: Nottingham Transport Heritage Centre, Mere Way, Ruddington, Nottingham NG11 6NX
Telephone Nº: (0115) 940-5705
Fax Nº: (0115) 940-5905
Year Formed: 1990 (Opened in 1994)
Location of Line: Ruddington to Loughborough Junction
Length of Line: 9 miles
Nº of Steam Locos: 6
Nº of Other Locos: 7
Nº of Members: 850
Annual Membership Fee: £10.00
Approx Nº of Visitors P.A.: 15,000

GENERAL INFORMATION

Nearest Railtrack Station: Nottingham (5 miles)
Nearest Bus Station: Bus service from Nottingham to the Centre
Car Parking: Free parking at site
Coach Parking: Free parking at site
Souvenir Shop(s): Yes
Food & Drinks: Yes

SPECIAL INFORMATION

The Heritage Centre covers an area of over eleven acres and is set within the Rushcliffe Country Park in Ruddington. Trains now run to Gotham Moor.

OPERATING INFORMATION

Opening Times: Sundays and Bank Holidays from 31st March to 28th October. Open 10.45am to 5.30pm. Also open for Santa Specials on December weekends.
Steam Working: Steam service runs from 11.30am
Prices: Adult £4.50
Child £2.50
Senior Citizens £4.00
Family £12.50 (2 adults + 3 children)

Web Site: www.nthc.org.uk

Detailed Directions by Car:
From All Parts: The centre is situated off the A60 Nottingham to Loughborough Road and is signposted just south of the traffic lights at Ruddington.

Paignton & Dartmouth Steam Railway

Address: Queen's Park Station, Torbay Road, Paignton TQ4 6AF	**Nº of Steam Locos**: 5
	Nº of Other Locos: 3
Telephone Nº: (01803) 555872	**Nº of Members**: –
Year Formed: 1973	**Annual Membership Fee**: –
Location of Line: Paignton to Kingswear	**Approx Nº of Visitors P.A.**: 350,000
Length of Line: 7 miles	**Gauge**: Standard

GENERAL INFORMATION

Nearest Railtrack Station: Paignton (adjacent)
Nearest Bus Station: Paignton (2 minutes walk)
Car Parking: Multi-storey or Railtrack car park
Coach Parking: Multi-storey (3 minutes walk)
Souvenir Shop(s): Yes – at Paignton & Kingswear
Food & Drinks: Yes – at Paignton & Kinswear

SPECIAL INFORMATION

A passenger ferry is available from Kingswear Station across to Dartmouth. Combined excursions are also available including train and river trips.

Web site: www.paignton-steamrailway.co.uk

OPERATING INFORMATION

Opening Times: Open daily from June to September (inclusive). Also open days in April, May, October and December (phone for details).
Steam Working: Trains run throughout the day from 10.30am to 5.00pm
Prices: Adult Return £6.60
 Child Return £4.60
Family Return £20.00 (2 adults + 2 children)

Detailed Directions by Car:
From All Parts: Take the M5 to Exeter and then the A380 to Paignton.

PEAK RAIL PLC

Address: Matlock Station, Matlock, Derbyshire DE4 3NA
Telephone Nº: (01629) 580381
Fax Nº: (01629) 760645
Year Formed: 1975
Location of Line: Matlock Riverside to Rowsley South

Length of Line: 4½ miles
Nº of Steam Locos: 3
Nº of Other Locos: 5
Nº of Members: 1,500
Annual Adult Membership Fee: £12.00
Approx Nº of Visitors P.A.: 30,000
Gauge: Standard

GENERAL INFORMATION

Nearest Railtrack Station: Matlock (500 yards)
Nearest Bus Station: Matlock
Car Parking: Paid car parking at Matlock Station, 200 spaces at Rowsley South Station, 20 spaces at Darley Dale Station
Coach Parking: Free parking at Rowsley South
Souvenir Shop(s): Yes
Food & Drinks: Yes

SPECIAL INFORMATION

The Palatine Restaurant Car is available whilst travelling on the train and caters for Sunday Lunches, Saturday Evening Meals and Party Bookings. Coach parties are welcomed for afternoon teas when the railway is operating.

OPERATING INFORMATION

Opening Times: Sundays in January-March and November. Weekends during the rest of the year. Also Wednesdays June and July, Tuesdays in July, Tuesdays and Wednesdays in August.
Steam Working: All services throughout the year.
Prices: Adult Return £6.00
Senior Citizen Return £4.00
Children (age 5-11) £1.00 (Under-5's free)
Family Ticket (2 adults + 2 children) £20.00

Detailed Directions by Car:
Exit the M1 at Junctions 28, 29 or 30 and follow signs towards Matlock. From North and South take A6 direct to Matlock. From Stoke-on-Trent, take the A52 to Ashbourne, then the A5035 to Matlock. Upon reaching Matlock follow the brown tourist signs.

PONTYPOOL & BLAENAVON RAILWAY

Address: c/o Council Offices, 101 High Street, Blaenavon, Torfaen NP4 9PT
Telephone Nº: (01495) 792263 or 760242
Year Formed: 1980 (Opened 1984)
Location of Line: Just off the B4248 between Blaenavon and Brynmawr
Length of Line: ¾ mile

Nº of Steam Locos: 10
Nº of Other Locos: 6
Nº of Members: 190
Annual Membership Fee: £10.00
Approx Nº of Visitors P.A.: 8,000
Gauge: Standard
Web site: www.pontypool-and-blaenavon.co.uk

GENERAL INFORMATION

Nearest Railtrack Station: Abergavenny (5 miles)
Nearest Bus Station: Blaenavon Town (1½ miles) – regular bus service within ¼ mile (except Sundays)
Car Parking: Free parking for 50 cars on site
Coach Parking: Available on site
Souvenir Shop(s): Yes – on the train (usually) and also a shop at 13 Broad Street, Blaenavon
Food & Drinks: Light refreshments on the train

SPECIAL INFORMATION

The railway operates over very steep gradients, is run entirely by volunteers and is the highest standard gauge preserved railway in Wales.

OPERATING INFORMATION

Opening Times: Every Sunday and Bank Holiday Monday from Easter to the end of September. Santa Specials and other Special events also run. Please phone the Railway for details. DMU services run on the first Saturday of each summer month and on Good Friday and Easter Saturday.
Steam Working: When working, a half-hourly service runs between 11.30am and 4.30pm.
Prices: Adult £2.40 (unlimited travel
Child £1.20 on the day of issue
Family £6.00 with ordinary returns)
Fares and conditions can vary for Special Events.

Detailed Directions by Car:
From All Parts: The railway is situated just off the B4248 between Blaenavon and Brynmawr and is well signposted as you approach Blaenavon. Use Junction 25A if using the M4 from the East, or Junction 26 from the West. Head for Pontypool. From the Midlands use the M50, A40 then A465 to Brynmawr. From North & West Wales consider using the 'Heads of the Valleys' A465 to Brynmawr. As you approach the Railway, look out for the Colliery water tower – you can't miss it!

RAILWAY PRESERVATION SOCIETY OF IRELAND

Address: Castleview, Whitehead,
Co. Antrim, Northern Ireland BT38 9NA
Telephone No: (028) 2826-0803
Year Formed: 1964
Location of Line: Whitehead, Co. Antrim
Length of Line: ¼ mile
Gauge: Irish Standard

No of Steam Locos: 9
No of Other Locos: 2
No of Members: 1,000
Annual Membership Fee: Adult £20.00;
Senior £12.00; Junior £10.00; Family £48.00
Approx No of Visitors P.A.: 10,000
Web Site: www.rpsi-online.org
E-mail: rpsitrains@hotmail.com

GENERAL INFORMATION

Nearest NIR Station: Whitehead (½ mile)
Nearest Bus Station: Whitehead (½ mile)
Car Parking: Free parking at site
Coach Parking: Free parking at site
Souvenir Shop(s): Yes
Food & Drinks: Yes

SPECIAL INFORMATION

The Society is the only Main Line Steam Operator in
Ireland.

OPERATING INFORMATION

Opening Times: Sundays in the Summer and also
during Easter and Christmas. There is also a regular
timetable of main line excursions. Phone for further
details.
Steam Working: 2.00pm to 5.00pm at Whitehead
Prices: Depends on the event or the destination of
main line excursions

Detailed Directions by Car:
Whitehead is situated about 15 miles to the North of Belfast just off the A2 between Larne and Carrickfergus. The
location is clearly signposted in Whitehead.

RAVENGLASS & ESKDALE RAILWAY

Address: Ravenglass, Cumbria
CA18 1SW
Telephone Nº: (01229) 717171
Year Formed: 1875
Location: The Lake District National Park
Length of Line: 7 miles

Gauge: 15 inches
Nº of Steam Locos: 6
Nº of Other Locos: 8
Nº of Members: 2,100
Approx Nº of Visitors P.A.: 250,000
Web site: www.ravenglass-railway.co.uk

GENERAL INFO

Nearest Railtrack Station: Ravenglass (adjacent)
Nearest Bus Stop: Ravenglass
Car Parking: Available at both terminals
Coach Parking: At Ravenglass
Souvenir Shop(s): Yes
Food & Drinks: Yes

SPECIAL INFO

This railway travels from the Lake District coast to the foot of England's highest fells and is England's oldest narrow-gauge railway.

OPERATING INFO

Opening Times: The service runs daily from the end of March until the beginning of November. Also runs during selected weekends in the Winter. Open from 8.00am to 5.00pm
Steam Working: Most services are steam hauled.
Prices: Adult £7.40
Child £3.70
Senior Citizens £6.90
Family £18.50
(2 adults + 2 children)

Detailed Directions by Car:
The railway is situated just off the main A595 Western Lake District road.

ROMNEY, HYTHE & DYMCHURCH RAILWAY

Address: New Romney Station, New Romney, Kent TN28 8PL	**Nº of Steam Locos:** 11
Telephone Nº: (01797) 362353	**Nº of Other Locos:** 5
Year Formed: 1927	**Nº of Members:** 2,500
Location of Line: Approximately 4 miles south of Folkestone	**Annual Membership Fee:** Supporters association – Adult £12.00; Junior £7.50
Length of Line: 13½ miles	**Approx Nº of Visitors P.A.:** 150,000
	Gauge: 15 inches

GENERAL INFORMATION

Nearest Railtrack Station: Folkestone Central (4 miles)

Nearest Bus Station: Folkestone (then take bus to Hythe)

Car Parking: Available at all major stations

Coach Parking: At New Romney & Dungeness

Souvenir Shop(s): Yes – 4 at various stations

Food & Drinks: 2 Cafes serving food and drinks

SPECIAL INFORMATION

Opened in 1927 as 'The World's Smallest Public Railway'. Now the only 15" gauge tourist main line railway in the world. Double track, 6 stations.

OPERATING INFORMATION

Opening Times: A daily service runs from 23rd March to 29th September. Open at weekends in March and October and for Santa Specials in December.

Steam Working: All operational days.

Prices: Depend on length of journey. Maximums:
Adult £9.40
Child £4.70
Family £29.50 (2 adult + 3 children)

Web Site: http://www.rhdr.demon.co.uk

Detailed Directions by Car:
Exit the M20 at Junction 11 then follow signs to Hythe and the brown tourist signs for the railway. Alternatively, Take the A259 to New Romney and follow the brown tourist signs for the railway.

RUTLAND RAILWAY MUSEUM

Address: Cottesmore Iron Ore Mines
Siding, Ashwell Road, Cottesmore,
Oakham, Rutland   LE15 7BX
Telephone Nº: (01572) 813203
Year Formed: 1979
Location of Line: Between the villages of
Cottesmore and Ashwell

Length of Line: ½ mile
Nº of Steam Locos: 13
Nº of Other Locos: 26
Nº of Members: 150
Annual Membership Fee: £8.00
Approx Nº of Visitors P.A.: 8,000
Gauge: Standard

GENERAL INFORMATION

Nearest Railtrack Station: Oakham (4 miles)
Nearest Bus Station: Cottesmore or Ashwell (both
1½ miles)
Car Parking: Available at the site
Coach Parking: Limited space available at the site
Souvenir Shop(s): Yes – on operating days
Food & Drinks: Yes – on operating days

SPECIAL INFORMATION

The Museum is located at the end of the former
Ashwell-Cottesmore mineral branch and is based at
the former exchange sidings.

OPERATING INFORMATION

Opening Times: Most weekends throughout the
year for static viewing. 11.00am to 5.00pm
Steam Working: 31st March, 1st April, 5th/6th May,
2nd/3rd/16th June, 25th/26th August, 22nd
September, 8th/15th/22nd December.
Prices: Adult £3.00
            Child £2.00 (no charge for under 5's)
            Family £8.00
Prices are for admission to the site on operating days
only. Admission is free at other times. Special prices
apply to Santa Specials in December.

Detailed Directions by Car:
From All Parts: The Museum is situated 4 miles north of Oakham between Ashwell and Cottesmore. Follow the
brown tourist signs on the B668 Oakham to the A1 road.

Scottish Industrial Railway Centre

Address: Minnivey Colliery, Burnton, Dalmellington, Ayrshire KA6 7PU	**N° of Steam Locos**: 9
Telephone N°: (01292) 531144 (Weekdays)	**N° of Other Locos**: 26
(01292) 313579 (Evenings & Weekends)	**N° of Members**: 180
Year Formed: 1974	**Annual Membership Fee**: £10.00
Location of Line: Dalmellington, Ayrshire	**Approx N° of Visitors P.A.**: 3,500
Length of Line: ¾ mile	**Gauge**: Standard
	Web site: www.arpg.org.uk

GENERAL INFORMATION

Nearest Railtrack Station: Ayr (14 miles)
Nearest Bus Station: Ayr (14 miles) – ½ hourly service to Dalmellington
Car Parking: Available at the site
Coach Parking: Spaces for 2 coaches at the site
Souvenir Shop(s): Yes
Food & Drinks: Yes (limited) – Public House adjacent

SPECIAL INFORMATION

This is a live Steam Centre where locomotives and rolling stock from Scottish Industrial backgrounds can be seen at work in an authentic setting.

OPERATING INFORMATION

Opening Times: The Centre is open for static display, with limited facilities every Saturday from the beginning of June to the end of September. Steam days: 5th May; 2nd/3rd/30th June; 7th/14th/21st/28th July; 4th/11th/18th/25th August; 1st September.
Steam Working: 11.00am to 4.30pm
Prices: Adult £2.50
Child £1.50
Family Tickets £6.00

Detailed Directions by Car:
From All Parts: The site is signposted from the A713 Ayr to Castle Douglas road.

SEVERN VALLEY RAILWAY

Address: Railway Station, Bewdley, Worcestershire DY12 1BG
Telephone Nº: (01299) 403816
Year Formed: 1965
Location of Line: Kidderminster (Worcs.) to Bridgnorth (Shropshire)
Length of Line: 16 miles

Nº of Steam Locos: 27
Nº of Other Locos: 12
Nº of Members: 14,000
Annual Membership Fee: Adult £12.00
Approx Nº of Passengers P.A.: 230,000
Gauge: Standard
Web site: www.svr.co.uk

GENERAL INFO

Nearest Railtrack Station: Kidderminster (adjacent)
Nearest Bus Station: Kidderminster (500 yards)
Car Parking: Large car park at Kidderminster. Spaces also available at other stations.
Coach Parking: At Kidderminster
Souvenir Shop(s): At Kidderminster & Bridgnorth
Food & Drinks: Yes – on most trains. Also at Kidderminster, Bewdley and Bridgnorth

SPECIAL INFO

The SVR has numerous special events including an Autumn Steam Gala, 1940's weekend, Classic Vehicle Day and visits by Thomas the Tank Engine and Santa!

OPERATING INFO

Opening Times: Weekends throughout the year. Also daily from 4th May to 29th September.
Steam Working: Train times vary depending on timetable information. Phone for details.
Prices: Vary depending on the journey taken:
Family Day Rover £27.00
(2 adults + 4 children)

Detailed Directions by Car:
For Kidderminster take M5 and exit Junction 3 or Junction 6. Follow the brown tourist signs for the railway; From the South: Take the M40 then M42 to Junction 1 for the A448 from Bromsgrove to Kidderminster.

THE SHAKESPEARE EXPRESS

Address: Vintage Trains Ltd, 670 Warwick Road, Tyseley, Birmingham B11 2HL
Telephone Nº: (0121) 707-4696
Year Formed: 1999
Location of Line: Birmingham Snow Hill, Tyseley, Stratford-upon-Avon

Length of Line: Approximately 25 miles
Nº of Steam Locos: 1 different loco each week from Tyseley Locomotive Works
Approx Nº of Visitors P.A.: Not known
Gauge: Standard
Web site: www.vintagetrains.co.uk

GENERAL INFORMATION

Nearest Railtrack Station: Birmingham Snow Hill, Tyseley and Stratford-upon-Avon
Nearest Bus Station: Birmingham: Digbeth; Tyseley: Reddings Lane Stop; Stratford-upon-Avon: Stop outside of the station
Car Parking: 200 spaces at Tyseley site
Coach Parking: Spaces at Tyseley site
Souvenir Shop(s): Yes
Food & Drinks: Light refreshments on train

SPECIAL INFORMATION

England's fastest regular steam train runs on Summer Sundays to three destinations.

OPERATING INFORMATION

Opening Times: 2002: Sundays from 7th July to 8th September inclusive.
Steam Working: 10.35am and 2.35pm from Birmingham; 12.50pm and 4.50pm from Stratford-upon-Avon
Prices: Adult Return Ticket £15.00
One free child ticket with each adult ticket
Extra Child Return Tickets £5.00 each.
Any combination of single or return tickets available to or from all three destinations. Pre-book or buy tickets on the day – group bookings are welcome.

Detailed Directions by Car to Tyseley Site:
From the North: Exit the M6 at Junction 6 and take A41 ring road towards Solihull; From the South: Exit the M42 at Junction 5 and take the A41 towards Birmingham.

SITTINGBOURNE & KEMSLEY LIGHT RAILWAY

Address: P.O. Box 300, Sittingbourne, Kent ME10 2DZ
Telephone Nº: (07944) 135033
Talking Timetable: (01795) 424899
E-mail: sklr@talk21.com
Year Formed: 1969
Location of Line: North of Sittingbourne

Length of Line: 2 miles
Nº of Steam Locos: 8
Nº of Other Locos: 3
Nº of Members: 250
Annual Membership Fee: £10.00
Approx Nº of Visitors P.A.: 10,000
Gauge: 2 feet 6 inches

GENERAL INFORMATION

Nearest Railtrack Station: Sittingbourne (¼ mile)
Nearest Bus Station: Sittingbourne Railtrack station
Car Parking: Available at Sittingbourne Station
Coach Parking: Available at Sittingbourne Station
Souvenir Shop(s): Yes
Food & Drinks: Yes

SPECIAL INFORMATION

The railway is the only preserved narrow gauge steam railway in S.E. England (formerly the Bowaters Paper Company Railway).

OPERATING INFORMATION

Opening Times: 29th March to 29th September, Sundays and Bank Holiday weekends. Also open on Wednesdays in the School holidays.
Steam Working: Trains run from 1.00pm normally, but from 11.00am on Bank Holidays weekends and Sundays in August. Last train runs at 4.00pm.
Prices: Adult £3.60
Child £2.00
Senior Citizens £2.50
Family £9.95

Detailed Directions by Car:
From East or West: Take the M2 (or M20) to A249 and travel towards Sittingbourne. Take the A2 to Sittingbourne town and continue to the roundabout outside the Railtrack station. Take the turning onto the B2006 (Milton Regis) and the car park entrance for the Railway is by the next roundabout, behind McDonalds.

Snowdon Mountain Railway

Address: Llanberis, Caernarfon, Gwynedd, Wales   LL55 4TY
Telephone Nº: (0870) 458-0033
Fax Nº: (01286) 872518
Year Formed: 1894
Location of Line: Llanberis to Snowdon summit

Length of Line: 4¾ miles
Nº of Steam Locos: 5
Nº of Other Locos: 4 + 3 Railcars
Nº of Members: –
Annual Membership Fee: –
Approx Nº of Visitors P.A.: 150,000
Gauge: 2 feet 7½ inches

GENERAL INFORMATION

Nearest Railtrack Station: Bangor (9 miles)
Nearest Bus Station: Caernarfon (7½ miles)
Car Parking: Llanberis Station car park – £3.00 Also other car parks nearby
Coach Parking: As above but space is very limited at busy times.
Souvenir Shop(s): Yes
Food & Drinks: Yes

SPECIAL INFORMATION

Britain's only public rack and pinion mountain railway. Climbs over 3,000 feet to Snowdon summit. Round trip approximately 2½ hours. Early and late in the season, the final section to the summit is closed and trains terminate lower down the mountain. Reduced fares then apply. Take a coat!

OPERATING INFORMATION

Opening Times: Open daily (weather permitting) from 15th March to 1st November. Trains run from 9.00am until mid/late afternoon. Subject to passenger demand.
Steam Working: Normally at least one steam loco on passenger service, but not guaranteed early or late in the season.
Prices: Adult £18.00   Child £13.00
Special rates for groups of 15 or more people.

Detailed Directions by Car:
Llanberis Station is situated on the A4086 Caernarfon to Capel Curig road, 7½ miles from Caernarfon. Convenient access via the main North Wales coast road (A55). Exit at the A55/A5 junction and follow signs to Llanberis via B4366, B4547 and A4086.

SOUTH DEVON RAILWAY

Address: Buckfastleigh Station, Buckfastleigh, Devon TQ11 0DZ	**N° of Steam Locos**: 16
Telephone N°: (0845) 345-1427	**N° of Other Locos**: 7
Year Formed: 1969	**N° of Members**: 1,300
Location of Line: Totnes to Buckfastleigh via Staverton	**Annual Membership Fee**: £13.00
	Approx N° of Visitors P.A.: 80,000
	Gauge: Standard
Length of Line: 7 miles	**Web Site**: www.southdevonrailway.org

GENERAL INFORMATION

Nearest Railtrack Station: Totnes (¼ mile)
Nearest Bus Station: Totnes (½ mile), Buckfastleigh (Station Road)
Car Parking: Free parking at Buckfastleigh, Council/BR parking at Totnes
Coach Parking: As above
Souvenir Shop(s): Yes – Buckfastleigh & on train
Food & Drinks: Yes – at Buckfastleigh & on train

SPECIAL INFORMATION

The railway was opened in 1872 as the Totnes, Buckfastleigh & Ashburton Railway.

OPERATING INFORMATION

Opening Times: Daily from 27th March to 27th October.
Steam Working: Almost all trains are steam hauled
Prices: Adult £6.80
    Child £4.00
    Family £19.60 (2 adults + 2 children)
N.B. Extra discounts are available for large groups

Detailed Directions by Car:
Buckfastleigh is half way between Exeter and Plymouth on the A38 Devon Expressway. Totnes can be reached by taking the A385 from Paignton and Torquay. Brown tourist signs give directions for the railway.

SOUTH DOWNS LIGHT RAILWAY

Address: South Downs Light Railway, Stopham Road, Pulborough RH20 1DS	**Nº of Steam Locos:** 10
Telephone Nº: (07711) 717470	**Nº of Other Locos:** 3
Year Formed: 1999	**Nº of Members:** 50
Location: Pulborough Garden Centre	**Annual Membership Fee:** Adult £25.00
Length of Line: ½ mile	**Approx Nº of Visitors P.A.:** 12,000
	Gauge: 10¼ inches

GENERAL INFORMATION

Nearest Railtrack Station: Pulborough (½ mile)
Nearest Bus Station: Bus stop just outside Centre
Car Parking: Free parking on site
Coach Parking: Free parking on site
Souvenir Shop(s): Yes
Food & Drinks: Yes – in the Garden Restaurant

SPECIAL INFORMATION

The members of the Railway own and operate the largest collection of 10¼ inch gauge scale locomotives in the UK. The Railway is sited/run in conjunction with the Pulborough Garden Centre.

OPERATING INFORMATION

Opening Times: 10.30am to 4.30pm on Saturdays; 11.00am to 3.30pm on Sundays; 10.30am to 4.30pm on Bank Holidays; 10.30am to 4.30pm on Wednesdays in August.
Steam Working: All services are steam hauled.
Prices: Adult £0.80
Child £0.50
Under 3's travel free of charge.
Supersaver ticket provides 12 rides for the price of 10.

Detailed Directions by Car:
From All Parts: The Centre is situated on the A283, ½ mile west of Pulborough. Pulborough itself is on the A29 London to Bognor Regis Road.

SOUTH TYNEDALE RAILWAY

Address: The Railway Station, Alston, Cumbria CA9 3JB	**Length of Line**: 2¼ miles
Telephone N°: (01434) 381696 (Enquiries) (01434) 382828 (Talking timetable)	**N° of Steam Locos**: 4
Year Formed: 1973	**N° of Other Locos**: 5
Location of Line: From Alston, northwards along South Tyne Valley to Kirkhaugh	**N° of Members**: 290
	Annual Membership Fee: £12.00
	Approx N° of Visitors P.A.: 22,000
	Gauge: 2 feet

GENERAL INFORMATION

Nearest Railtrack Station: Haltwhistle (15 miles)
Nearest Bus Station: Alston Townfoot (¼ mile)
Car Parking: Free parking at Alston Station
Coach Parking: Free parking at Alston Station
Souvenir Shop(s): Yes
Food & Drinks: Yes

Web site: www.strps.org.uk

OPERATING INFORMATION

Opening Times: Weekends from the 29th March to 27th October. Open daily from 20th July to 1st September. Also open on various other dates – contact the Railway for further details.
Steam Working: Varies, but generally weekends & Bank Holidays throughout the Summer & December weekends. Also daily from 21st July to 1st September.
Prices: Adult Return £4.00; Single £2.50
          Child Return £2.00; Single £1.50
          Children under 3 travel free
          Adult All Day Ticket £10.00
          Child All Day Ticket £5.00

Detailed Directions by Car:
Alston can be reached by a number of roads from various directions including A689, A686 and the B6277. Alston Station is situated just off the A686 Hexham road, north of Alston Town Centre. Look for the brown tourist signs on roads into Alston.

SPA VALLEY RAILWAY

Address: West Station, Tunbridge Wells, Kent TN2 5QY	**Nº of Steam Locos**: 6
	Nº of Other Locos: 8
Telephone Nº: (01892) 537715	**Nº of Members**: Approximately 660
Year Formed: 1985	**Annual Membership Fee**: £13.50
Location of Line: Tunbridge Wells West to Eridge (currently to Groombridge)	**Approx Nº of Visitors P.A.**: 20,000
	Gauge: Standard
Length of Line: 3½ miles operational	**Web Site**: www.spavalleyrailway.co.uk

GENERAL INFORMATION

Nearest Railtrack Station: Tunbridge Wells Central (½ mile)
Nearest Bus Stop: Outside Sainsbury's (100yds)
Car Parking: Available nearby
Coach Parking: Coach station in Montacute Road (150 yards)
Souvenir Shop(s): Yes
Food & Drinks: Yes

SPECIAL INFORMATION

The Railway's Tunbridge Wells Terminus is in a historic and unique L.B. & S.C.R. engine shed. The Railway's aims are to extend to Eridge to connect with the Main Line.

OPERATING INFORMATION

Opening Times: Weekends from March to October. Some weekdays during School Holidays and also Santa Specials in December.
Steam Working: Most services are steam-hauled. Trains run from 10.30am to 4.15pm.
Prices: Adult Return £4.00
Child/Senior Citizen Return £3.00
Unlimited Day Travel £6.00
Family Return £12.00 (2 adult + 2 child)
Parties of 20 or more are charged at £3.50 per head.

Detailed Directions by Car:
The Spa Valley Railway is in the southern part of Tunbridge Wells, 100 yards off the A26. Station is adjacent to Sainsbury's and Homebase. Car Parks are nearby in Major Yorks Road, Union House & Linden Close.

STEAM – MUSEUM OF THE GREAT WESTERN RAILWAY

Address: Steam – Museum of the Great Western Railway, Kemble Drive, Swindon   SN2 2TA
Telephone Nº: (01793) 466646
Year Formed: 2000

Nº of Steam Locos: 4
Nº of Other Locos: –
Approx Nº of Visitors P.A.: 150,000
Web site: www.steam-museum.org.uk

GENERAL INFORMATION

Nearest Railtrack Station: Swindon (10 min. walk)
Nearest Bus Station: Swindon (10 minute walk)
Car Parking: Ample parking space available in the Outlet Centre (charges apply)
Coach Parking: Free parking on site
Souvenir Shop(s): Yes
Food & Drinks: Yes

SPECIAL INFORMATION

Voted Wiltshire's Family Attraction of the Year, STEAM tells the story of the men and women who built the Great Western Railway.

OPERATING INFORMATION

Opening Times: Open all year round from 10.00am to 5.00pm Monday to Saturday, 11.00am to 5.00pm on Sundays. During the Summer months, the Museum is open until 5.30pm.
Steam Working: –
Prices: Adult Tickets £5.70
         Child Tickets £3.60
         Family Tickets £14.00
         Children under 5 are admitted free

Detailed Directions by Car:
Exit the M4 at Junction 16 and follow the brown tourist signs to 'Outlet Centre'. Similarly follow the brown signs from all other major routes.   From the Railway Station: STEAM is a short walk and is accessible through the pedestrian tunnel – entrance by Emlyn Square.

STRATHSPEY STEAM RAILWAY

Address: Aviemore Station, Dalfaber Road, Aviemore, Inverness-shire, PH22 1PY	**Length of Line:** 5½ miles at present
	Gauge: Standard
Telephone N°: (01479) 810725	**N° of Steam Locos:** 7
Year Formed: 1971	**N° of Other Locos:** 6
Location of Line: Aviemore to Boat of Garten and Broomhill, Inverness-shire	**N° of Members:** 800
	Annual Membership Fee: £16.00
	Approx N° of Visitors P.A.: 45,000

GENERAL INFO

Nearest Railtrack Station: Aviemore – Strathspey trains depart from Platform 3
Nearest Bus Station: Aviemore (600 yds)
Car Parking: Available at all stations
Coach Parking: Available at Aviemore and Boat of Garten Stations
Souvenir Shop(s): Yes – at Aviemore and Boat of Garten Stations
Food & Drinks: Available on Steam trains only (except on Saturdays)

SPECIAL INFO

The railway now operates from Aviemore Station. In the waiting room, there is a small exhibition about the history of the line between Aviemore & Inverness and about the renovation of the station. The Railway is extending to Broomhill Station on 1st June 2002 subject to approval by H.M. Railway Inspectorate.

OPERATING INFO

Opening Times: Daily from 26th May to 30th September. Restricted days in October and other dates in December. Phone for details. Generally open from 9.30am to 4.30pm.
Steam Working: Most trains are steam-hauled but diesel power is used whenever necessary. Phone the Railway for details.
Prices: Adult Return £6.00
 Child Return £3.00
 Family Return £15.00
 (2 adults + up to 3 children)
Day Rover tickets are available
Note: Prices will increase once the Railway has extended to Broomhill.

Detailed Directions by Car:
For Aviemore Station from South: Take the A9 then B970 and turn left between the railway & river bridges. For Boat of Garten from North; Take the A9 then A938 to Carr Bridge, then B9153 and A95 and follow the signs; From North East: Take A95 to Boat of Garten.

SWANAGE RAILWAY

Address: Station House, Railway Station, Swanage, Dorset BH19 1HB	**N° of Steam Locos**: 8
Telephone N°: (01929) 425800	**N° of Other Locos**: 3
Year Formed: 1976	**N° of Members**: 4,200
Location of Line: Swanage to Norden	**Annual Membership Fee**: Adult £15.00; Junior & Senior Citizens £9.00
Length of Line: 6 miles	**Approx N° of Visitors P.A.**: 180,911
Gauge: Standard	(exact figures for 2001)

GENERAL INFORMATION

Nearest Railtrack Station: Wareham (10 miles)
Nearest Bus Station: Swanage Station (adjacent)
Car Parking: Park & Ride at Norden. Public car parks in Swanage (5 minutes walk)
Coach Parking: Available at Norden
Souvenir Shop(s): Yes – at Swanage Station
Food & Drinks: Yes – buffet available on trains and also Swanage Station Buffet.

SPECIAL INFORMATION

The railway runs along part of the route of the old Swanage to Wareham railway, opened in 1885.

OPERATING INFORMATION

Opening Times: Weekends throughout the year and daily from April to October. Opens from 9.30am to 5.00pm.
Steam Working: All services are steam-hauled
Prices: Adult £6.00
Child £4.00
Family £18.00

Detailed Directions by Car:
Norden Park & Ride Station is situated off the A351 on the approach to Corfe Castle. Swanage Station is situated in the centre of the town, just a few minutes walk from the beach. Take the A351 to reach Swanage.

Swansea Vale Railway

Address: Upper Bank Works, Pentrechwyth, Swansea SA1 7DB	**Nº of Steam Locos:** 5
Telephone Nº: (01792) 461000	**Nº of Other Locos:** 3
Year Formed: 1980	**Nº of Members:** 150
Location of Line: Six Pit Junction, Llansamlet, Swansea	**Annual Membership Fee:** £10.00
Length of Line: ¾ mile	**Approx Nº of Visitors P.A.:** 5,000
	Gauge: Standard
	Web: homepage.ntlworld.com/michael.meyrick

GENERAL INFORMATION

Nearest Railtrack Station: Llansamlet (¾ mile)
Nearest Bus Station: Swansea Quadrant (3 miles)
Car Parking: 150 spaces available at the site
Coach Parking: 3 spaces available at the site
Souvenir Shop(s): Yes – on the trains
Food & Drinks: Light snacks are available on trains

SPECIAL INFORMATION

The line is due to be extended to 1¼ miles in the Autumn of 1999. Also, guided tours can be arranged at £1.00 per head to view the shed, old turntable base and ash pit.

OPERATING INFORMATION

Opening Times: Saturdays between April and September. Also Bank Holidays and a number of other dates. Not always a steam service. Contact the railway for more complete information. Services run from 12.00pm to 4.00pm.
Steam Working: Certain dates only, although most running days in the Summer are Steam days. Contact the railway for more information.
Prices: Adult £3.00
         Child £2.00
         Family £12.00
Pay once – ride all day.
Prices may change for special events.

Detailed Directions by Car:
From the East: Exit the M4 at Junction 44 (Swansea East), follow signs for Llansamlet and Morriston. At the third set of traffic lights turn left and look for the steam loco signs; From the West: Exit the M4 at Junction 45 (Morriston) then follow signs for Llansamlet; From City Centre: Cross the river near Parc Tawe Shopping Centre, follow signs to Llansamlet on A4217 for 3 miles. Pass the Colliers Arms on the left, pass under the main line railway bridge and turn next left.

SWINDON & CRICKLADE RAILWAY

Address: Blunsdon Station, Tadpole Lane, Blunsdon, Swindon, Wilts SN25 2DA	**N° of Steam Locos**: 8
Phone N°: (01793) 771615	**N° of Other Locos**: 7
Year Formed: 1978	**N° of Members**: 350
Location of Line: Blunsdon to Hayes Knoll	**Annual Membership Fee**: £10.00
Length of Line: ¾ mile	**Approx N° of Visitors P.A.**: 5,000
	Gauge: Standard

GENERAL INFORMATION

Nearest Railtrack Station: Swindon (5 miles)
Nearest Bus Station: Bus stop in Blunsdon (1 mile)
Car Parking: Free parking available at Blunsdon
Coach Parking: Free parking at Blunsdon
Souvenir Shop(s): Yes
Food & Drinks: Yes

SPECIAL INFORMATION

The Engine Shed and Hayes Knoll Station has just opened to the public.

Web site: www.swindon-cricklade-railway.org

OPERATING INFORMATION

Opening Times: The Railway is open every weekend and Bank Holidays for viewing only. Santa Specials in December and other various special events throughout the year have train rides. Open 11.00am to 4.00pm. Diesel trains run every Sunday.
Steam Working: Certain dates only – contact the railway for further details.
Prices: Adult £3.00
         Child £2.00
         Family £9.00
Prices are different for special events.

Detailed Directions by Car:
From the M4: Exit the M4 at Junction 15 and follow the A419. After the roundabout by the Little Chef, turn left at the next set of traffic lights towards Blunsdon Station and follow the signs: From Cirencester: Follow the A419 to the traffic lights at the top of Blunsdon Hill, then turn right and follow signs for the railway.

TALYLLYN RAILWAY

Address: Wharf Station, Tywyn, Gwynedd, LL36 9EY	**Nº of Steam Locos**: 6
Telephone Nº: (01654) 710472	**Nº of Other Locos**: 4
Year Formed: 1865	**Nº of Members**: 3,500
Location of Line: Tywyn to Nant Gwernol Station	**Annual Membership Fee**: Adult £20.00
Length of Line: 7¼ miles	**Approx Nº of Visitors P.A.**: 50,000
	Gauge: 2 feet 3 inches
	Web site: www.talyllyn.co.uk

GENERAL INFORMATION

Nearest Railtrack Station: Tywyn (300 yards)
Nearest Bus Station: Tywyn (300 yards)
Car Parking: 100 yards away
Coach Parking: Free parking (100 yards)
Souvenir Shop(s): Yes
Food & Drinks: Yes

SPECIAL INFORMATION

Talyllyn Railway was the first preserved railway in the world – saved from closure in 1951. The railway was opened in 1866 to carry slate from Bryn Eglwys Quarry to Tywyn.

OPERATING INFORMATION

Opening Times: Daily from 24th March to 2nd November. Generally open from 10.00am to 5.00pm (later during the summer).
Steam Working: All passenger trains are steam-hauled.
Prices: Adult Return £9.50 (Day Rover ticket) Children (ages 5-15) pay £2.00 if travelling with an adult. Otherwise, they pay half adult fare. Children under the age of 5 travel free of charge.
The fares shown above are for a full round trip. Tickets to intermediate stations are cheaper.

Detailed Directions by Car:
From the North: Take the A493 from Dolgellau into Tywyn; From the South: Take the A493 from Machynlleth to Tywyn.

TANFIELD RAILWAY

Address: Marley Hill Engine Shed, Old Marley Hill, Gateshead, Tyne & Wear NE16 5ET **Telephone Nº**: (0191) 388-7545 **Fax Nº**: (0191) 387-4784 **Year Formed**: 1976 **Location of Line**: Between Sunniside & East Tanfield, Co. Durham	**Length of Line**: 3 miles **Nº of Steam Locos**: 25 **Nº of Other Locos**: 9 **Nº of Members**: 150 **Annual Membership Fee**: £7.00 **Approx Nº of Visitors P.A.**: 40,000 **Gauge**: Standard **Web site**: www.tanfield-railway.co.uk

GENERAL INFORMATION

Nearest Railtrack Station: Newcastle-upon-Tyne (8 miles)
Nearest Bus St'n: Gateshead Interchange (6 miles)
Car Parking: Spaces for 150 cars at St. Andrews House and 100 spaces at East Tanfield
Coach Parking: Spaces for 6 or 7 coaches only
Souvenir Shop(s): Yes
Food & Drinks: Yes – light snacks only

SPECIAL INFORMATION

Tanfield Railway is the oldest existing railway in use – it was originally opened in 1725. It also runs beside The Causey Arch, the oldest railway bridge in the world.

OPERATING INFORMATION

Opening Times: Every Sunday & Bank Holiday Monday throughout the year. Also opens on Wednesdays & Thursdays in Summer school holidays.
Steam Working: Trains run 11.00am to 4.00pm (11.30am to 3.15pm in the Winter).
Prices: Adult £4.00
  Child £2.00 (Under 5's travel free)
  Family £10.00 (2 adults + 2 children)

Detailed Directions by Car:
Sunniside Station is off the A6076 Sunniside to Stanley road in Co. Durham. To reach the Railway, leave A1(M), follow signs for Beamish museum at Chester-le-Street then continue to Stanley and follow Tanfield Railway signs.

TEIFI VALLEY RAILWAY

Address: Henllan Station, Henllan, near Newcastle Emlyn, Carmarthenshire
Telephone Nº: (01559) 371077
Year Formed: 1972
Location of Line: Between Cardigan and Carmarthen off the A484
Length of Line: 2 miles

Nº of Steam Locos: 2
Nº of Other Locos: 3
Nº of Members: Approximately 150
Annual Membership Fee: £12.00
Approx Nº of Visitors P.A.: 15,000
Gauge: 2 feet
Web site: www.teifivr.f9.co.uk

GENERAL INFORMATION

Nearest Railtrack Station: Carmarthen (10 miles)
Nearest Bus Station: Carmarthen (10 miles)
Car Parking: Spaces for 70 cars available.
Coach Parking: Spaces for 4 coaches available.
Souvenir Shop(s): Yes
Food & Drinks: Yes (snacks only)

SPECIAL INFORMATION

The Railway was formerly part of the G.W.R. but now runs on a Narrow Gauge using Quarry Engines.

OPERATING INFORMATION

Opening Times: Open daily from Easter until the end of October (closed most Fridays and Saturdays). Open every day from 14th July to 5th September. Open on some days in December for 'Santa Specials'. Open 10.00am – 3.30pm when the last train departs.
Steam Working: Occasional steam working – please phone the Railway for details.
Prices: Adult £5.00
Child £3.00
Senio Citizens £4.00
A 10% discount is available for parties of 10 or more.

Detailed Directions by Car:
From All Parts: The Railway is situated in the Village of Henllan between the A484 and the A475 (on the B4334) about 4 miles east of Newcastle Emlyn.

TELFORD STEAM RAILWAY

Address: The Old Loco Shed, Bridge Road, Horsehay, Telford, Shropshire
Telephone Nº: (01952) 503880
Enquiries: (07765) 858348
Year Formed: 1976
Location of Line: Based at Horsehay & Dawley Station

Length of Line: ½ mile standard gauge, an eighth of a mile 2 foot narrow gauge
Nº of Steam Locos: 6
Nº of Other Locos: 8
Nº of Members: Approximately 180
Annual Membership Fee: £8.50
Approx Nº of Visitors P.A.: 10,000

GENERAL INFORMATION

Nearest Railtrack Station: Wellington or Telford Central
Nearest Bus Station: Dawley (1 mile)
Car Parking: Free parking at the site
Coach Parking: Free parking at the site
Souvenir Shop(s): 'Freight Stop Gift Shop'
Food & Drinks: 'The Furnaces' Tea Room

SPECIAL INFORMATION

Telford Steam Railway has both a Standard Gauge and Narrow Gauge line as well as Miniature and Model Railways.

OPERATING INFORMATION

Opening Times: Every Sunday and Bank Holiday between Easter and the end of September. Santa Specials run in December. Open 11.00am to 4.00pm except Bank Holidays when it is open until 5.00pm
Steam Working: 2 foot gauge on all operating days. Standard gauge on the last Sunday of the month and also on Bank Holidays.
Prices: Adult all day tickets £3.50
              Child all day tickets £2.50

Detailed Directions by Car:
From All Parts: Exit the M54 at Junction 6 and follow the brown tourist signs for the railway.

TYSELEY LOCOMOTIVE WORKS VISITOR CENTRE

Address: 670 Warwick Road, Tyseley, Birmingham B11 2HL
Telephone Nº: (0121) 707-4696
Year Formed: 1969
Location of Museum: Tyseley
Length of Line: A third of a mile

Nº of Steam Locos: Varies with visiting Locos and restoration contracts
Nº of Members: Approximately 600
Approx Nº of Visitors P.A.: 15,000
Gauge: Standard
Web site: www.vintagetrains.co.uk

GENERAL INFORMATION

Nearest Railtrack Station: Tyseley (5 mins. walk)
Nearest Bus Station: Birmingham. Bus Stop at Reddings Lane – 2 minutes walk (Bus route 37 passes the entrance)
Car Parking: 200 spaces at Railway site
Coach Parking: Space at Railway site
Souvenir Shop(s): Yes
Food & Drinks: Yes

SPECIAL INFORMATION

The Museum runs a large workshop which produces refurbished locomotives. Driver training courses are available on most weekends – bookings for these courses are essential.

OPERATING INFORMATION

Opening Times: Bank Holidays and Weekends only. Open from 10.00am to 4.00pm in the Winter, 10.00am to 5.00pm in the Summer.
Steam Working: On the days of driving course operations only.
Prices: Adult £2.50
Child £1.25
Family £6.25

Detailed Directions by Car:
From the North: Exit the M6 at Junction 6 and take A41 ring road towards Solihull; From the South: Exit the M42 at Junction 5 and take the A41 towards Birmingham.

VALE OF GLAMORGAN RAILWAY

Address: Barry Island Station, Barry Island, Vale of Glamorgan CF62 5TH	**N⁰ of Steam Locos**: 5 (10 in storage)
Telephone N⁰: (01446) 748816	**N⁰ of Other Locos**: 3
Year Formed: 1979 (1994 on present site)	**N⁰ of Members**: 250
Location of Line: Barry Island	**Annual Membership Fee**: £7.00
Length of Line: 1¼ miles	**Approx N⁰ of Visitors P.A.**: 10,000
	Gauge: Standard

GENERAL INFO

Nearest Railtrack Station: Barry Island (across the platform)
Nearest Bus Station: Outside station
Car Parking: Large car park (300 yards)
Coach Parking: Car park (300 yards)
Souvenir Shop(s): Yes
Food & Drinks: Yes

SPECIAL INFO

The aim of the company is to portray the rich history of railways in South Wales.

OPERATING INFO

Opening Times: Weekends from mid July until early September. Special events will run at Easter, during the Jubilee and Santa Specials at Christmas. Please phone the Railway for details.
Steam Working: 11.00am to 4.00pm
Prices: Adult £3.00
Child £2.00
Family £7.00
(2 adults + 2 children)

Detailed Directions by Car:
Exit the M4 at Junction 33 and follow the brown tourist signs for the funfair and beach to Barry Island. The station is situated on the left behind the funfair.

VALE OF RHEIDOL RAILWAY

Address: The Locomotive Shed, Park Avenue, Aberystwyth, Dyfed   SY23 1PG
Telephone Nº: (01970) 625819
Year Formed: 1902
Location of Line: Aberystwyth to Devil's Bridge
Length of Line: 11¾ miles

Nº of Steam Locos: 3
Nº of Other Locos: 1
Nº of Members: None
Annual Membership Fee: –
Approx Nº of Visitors P.A.: 37,000
Gauge: 1 foot 11¾ inches
Web site: www.rheidolrailway.co.uk

GENERAL INFORMATION

Nearest Railtrack Station: Aberystwyth (adjacent)
Nearest Bus Station: Aberystwyth (adjacent)
Car Parking: 2 short stay + 2 long stay car parks within 400 yards.
Coach Parking: Parking available 400 yards away.
Souvenir Shop(s): Yes
Food & Drinks: Yes

SPECIAL INFORMATION

The journey between the stations take one hour in each direction. At Devil's Bridge there is a cafe, toilets, a picnic area and the famous Mynach Falls. The line climbs over 600 feet in 11¾ miles.

OPERATING INFORMATION

Opening Times: Open almost every day from 29th March to 26th October. Closed some Fridays in May and September and also Sundays and Fridays in October.
Steam Working: All trains are steam-hauled. Trains run from 10.30am to 4.00pm on most days.
Prices: Adult Return £11.00
Child Return – First 2 children per adult pay £2.00 each. Further children pay £5.50 each

---

Detailed Directions by Car:
From the North take A487 into Aberystwyth. From the East take A470 and A44 to Aberystwyth. From the South take A487 or A485 to Aberystwyth. The Station is joined on to the Railtrack Station in Alexandra Road.

WELLS & WALSINGHAM LIGHT RAILWAY

Address: The Station, Wells-next-the-Sea NR23 1QB
Telephone Nº: (01328) 710631
Year Formed: 1982
Location of Line: Wells-next-the-Sea to Walsingham, Norfolk
Length of Line: 4 miles

Nº of Steam Locos: 1
Nº of Other Locos: 1
Nº of Members: 50
Annual Membership Fee: £11.00
Approx Nº of Visitors P.A.: 20,000
Gauge: 10¼ inches

GENERAL INFORMATION

Nearest Railtrack Station: King's Lynn (21 miles)
Nearest Bus Station: Norwich (24 miles)
Car Parking: Free parking at site
Coach Parking: Free parking at site
Souvenir Shop(s): Yes
Food & Drinks: Yes

SPECIAL INFORMATION

The Railway is the longest 10¼ inch narrow-gauge steam railway in the world. The course of the railway is famous for wildlife and butterflies in season.

OPERATING INFORMATION

Opening Times: Daily from Good Friday to the end of October.
Steam Working: Trains run from 10.15am on operating days.
Prices: Adult Return £6.00
Child Return £4.50

Detailed Directions by Car:
Wells-next-the-Sea is situated on the North Norfolk Coast midway between Hunstanton and Cromer. The Main Station is situated on the main A149 Stiffkey Road. Follow the brown tourist signs for the Railway.

WELSH HIGHLAND RAILWAY (CAERNARFON)

Postal Address: Ffestiniog Railway, Harbour Station, Porthmadog LL49 9NF
Telephone Nº: (01766) 516073
Web site: www.festrail.co.uk
Year Formed: 1997
Location: Caernarfon to Waunfawr
Length of Line: 7 miles

Nº of Steam Locos: 5
Nº of Other Locos: 2
Nº of Members: 1,000
Annual Membership Fee: £20.00
Approx Nº of Visitors P.A.: 70,000
Gauge: 1 foot 11½ inches

GENERAL INFORMATION

Nearest Railtrack Station: Bangor (7 miles) (Bus service Nº 5 runs to Caernarfon)
Nearest Bus Station: Caernarfon
Car Parking: Parking available at Caernarfon
Coach Parking: At Victoria Docks (¼ mile)
Souvenir Shop(s): Yes
Food & Drinks: Light refreshments on some trains

SPECIAL INFORMATION

The Railway is being reconstructed between Caernarfon and Porthmadog along the track bed of the original Welsh Highland Railway. A further extension from Waunfawr to Rhyd Ddu is due to open in 2002.

OPERATING INFORMATION

Opening Times: Daily from 31st March to 4th November + some trains in Winter. Train times vary.
Steam Working: Most trains in the Summer are steam-hauled.
Prices: Adult £8.00 to Waunfawr
Child £4.00 to Waunfawr

N.B. One Child is admitted free of charge with every Adult. Also, price reductions are available for Senior Citizens and groups of 20 or more.

Detailed Directions by Car:
Take either the A487(T), the A4085 or the A4086 to Caernarfon then follow the brown tourist signs for the Railway which is situated in St. Helens Road next to the Castle.

WELSH HIGHLAND RAILWAY (PORTHMADOG)

Address: Tremadog Road, Porthmadog, Gwynedd LL49 9DY	**Nº of Steam Locos**: 7
Telephone Nº: (01766) 513402	**Nº of Other Locos**: 18
Year Formed: 1964	**Nº of Members**: 1,200
Location of Line: Tremadog Road, Porthmadog, Gwynedd LL49 9DY	**Annual Membership Fee**: £10.00 Adult
	Approx Nº of Visitors P.A.: 20,000
	Gauge: 60 centimetres (2 foot)
Length of Line: ¾ mile	**Web site**: www.whr.co.uk

GENERAL INFORMATION

Nearest Railtrack Station: Porthmadog (50 yards)
Nearest Bus Station: Services 1 & 3 stop 200 yards away
Car Parking: Free parking at site, also 2 public car parks within 100 yards.
Coach Parking: Adjacent
Souvenir Shop(s): Yes – large range of books, videos and souvenirs.
Food & Drinks: Yes – excellent home cooking!

SPECIAL INFORMATION

The Welsh Highland Railway is a family-orientated attraction based around a Railway Heritage Centre and includes a tour of the sheds. A 2 mile extension to Pont Croesor is currently being constructed.

OPERATING INFORMATION

Opening Times: Open at Easter then during weekends in May. Opens daily from 1st June to 27th October then December weekends for Santa Specials.
Steam Working: Weekends then daily between 20th July and 1st September. Some other dates also. Trains run at 11.00am, 12.00pm, 2.00pm, 3.00pm & 4.00pm.
Prices: Adult Return £3.00
　　　　　Child Return £2.00
　　　　　Senior Citizen Return £2.50
　　　　　Family Return £7.50
　　　　　(2 adults + 2 children)
Children under 5 are admitted free of charge

Detailed Directions by Car:
From Bangor/Caernarfon take the A487 to Porthmadog. From Pwllheli take the A497 to Porthmadog then turn left at the roundabout. From the Midlands take A487 to Portmadog. Once in Porthmadog, follow the brown tourist signs. The line is located right next to Porthmadog Railtrack Station.

WELSHPOOL & LLANFAIR LIGHT RAILWAY

Address: The Station, Llanfair Caereinion,
Powys SY21 0SF
Telephone Nº: (01938) 810441
Year Formed: 1959
Location of Line: Welshpool to Llanfair
Caereinion, Mid Wales
Length of Line: 8 miles

Nº of Steam Locos: 7
Nº of Other Locos: 3
Nº of Members: 2,300
Annual Membership Fee: £17.50
Approx Nº of Visitors P.A.: 25,000
Gauge: 2 feet 6 inches

GENERAL INFORMATION

Nearest Railtrack Station: Welshpool (1 mile)
Nearest Bus Station: Welshpool (1 mile)
Car Parking: Free parking at Welshpool and
Llanfair Caereinion
Coach Parking: As above
Souvenir Shop(s): Yes – at both ends of line
Food & Drinks: Yes – at Llanfair only

SPECIAL INFORMATION

The railway has the steepest gradient of any British
railway, reaching a summit of 603 feet.

OPERATING INFORMATION

Opening Times: Easter and Bank Holidays and
weekends in April, May and September. Daily from
14th July to September 2nd. Most other days in June
and July plus dates in September, October and
December. Generally open from 9.30am to 6.00pm.
Steam Working: All trains are steam-hauled
Prices: Adult £8.50
    Senior Citizens £7.50
Children under the age of 3 are free of charges. The
first child aged 3-15 per adult is charged £1.00. All
other children are charged half-price fare of £4.25

Detailed Directions by Car:
Both stations are situated alongside the A458 Shrewsbury to Dolgellau road and are clearly signposted

---

WEST LANCASHIRE LIGHT RAILWAY

Address: Station Road, Hesketh Bank, Nr. Preston, Lancashire   PR4 6SP
Telephone Nº: (01772) 815881
Year Formed: 1967
Location of Line: On former site of Alty's Brickworks, Hesketh Bank
Length of Line: ¼ mile

Nº of Steam Locos: 9
Nº of Other Locos: 24
Nº of Members: Approximately 85
Annual Membership Fee: £10.00 Adult; £15.00 Family
Approx Nº of Visitors P.A.: 13,500

GENERAL INFORMATION

Nearest Railtrack Station: Rufford (4 miles)
Nearest Bus Station: Preston (7 miles)
Car Parking: Space for 50 cars at site
Coach Parking: Space for 3 coaches at site
Souvenir Shop(s): Yes
Food & Drinks: Only soft drinks & snacks

SPECIAL INFORMATION

The Railway is run by volunteers and there is a large collection of Industrial Narrow Gauge equipment.

Web site: www.djrl2ecg.demon.co.uk/wllr/wllr.html

OPERATING INFORMATION

Opening Times: Sundays and Bank Holidays throughout the year. No trains run from November to April (except Santa Specials). Various other Special Events are held during the Summer – phone for details. Trains run from 12.00pm to 5.20pm
Steam Working: Trains operate on Sundays and Bank Holidays from 29th March until the end of October. There are also 'Santa Specials' on the two weekends prior to Christmas.
Prices: Adult £1.75   Child £1.00
                   Family Tickets £4.50
                   Senior Citizens £1.50

Detailed Directions by Car:
Travel by the A59 from Liverpool or Preston or by the A565 from Southport to the junction of the two roads at Tarleton. From here follow signs to Hesketh Bank. The Railway is signposted.

WEST SOMERSET RAILWAY

Address: The Railway Station, Minehead, Somerset TA24 5BG	**Length of Line:** 19¾ miles
Telephone Nº: (01643) 704996 (enquiries), (01643) 707650 (Talking timetable)	**Nº of Steam Locos:** 9
	Nº of Other Locos: 13
Year Formed: 1976	**Nº of Members:** 4,000
Location of Line: Bishops Lydeard (near Taunton) to Minehead	**Annual Membership Fee:** £12.00
	Approx Nº of Visitors P.A.: 170,000
	Gauge: Standard

GENERAL INFORMATION

Nearest Railtrack Station: Taunton (4 miles)
Nearest Bus Station: Taunton (4½ miles) – Services 28, 28A & 928 run to Bishops Lydeard
Car Parking: Free parking at Bishops Lydeard; Council car parking at Minehead
Coach Parking: As above
Souvenir Shop(s): Yes – at Minehead, Bishops Lydeard and Washford
Food & Drinks: Yes – At some stations. Buffet and Dining cars on all trains.

SPECIAL INFORMATION

Britain's longest Heritage railway runs through the Quantock Hills & along Bristol Channel Coast. Ten Stations with museums at Washford & Blue Anchor.

OPERATING INFORMATION

Opening Times: March to December. Daily from May to September. Open 9.30am to 5.30pm
Steam Working: All operatings days except Diesel Galas.
Prices: Adult £9.80
 Child £4.90
 Family £26.00 (2 adults + 2 children – up to 3 additional children travel for £1.00 each)

Web site: www.west-somerset-railway.co.uk

Detailed Directions by Car:
Exit the M5 at Taunton (Junction 25) and follow signs for A358 to Williton and then the A39 for Minehead. In Minehead, brown tourist signs give directions to the railway.

RAILWAY CIGARETTE & TRADE CARDS

We have a limited stock of cigarette and trade cards available, postage free, as follows: –

Issuer	Year	Set	Qty.	Price
TADDY & CO.	1980	Railway Locomotives	26 std.	£5.00
HOBBYPRESS GUIDES	1984	Preserved Steam Railways 2nd	20 std.	£1.25
HOBBYPRESS GUIDES	1982	Victorian Steam Railway Miniprints	24 lge.	£7.50

SPECIAL OFFER – Buy all 3 of the above sets for just £12.00

Order from: –

Marksman Publications
72 St. Peters Avenue
Cleethorpes
N.E. Lincolnshire
DN35 8HU

The Bluebell Railway *(above)*
Bodmin & Wenford Railway *(below)*

Buckinghamshire Railway
Centre *(left)*

Bure Valley Railway *(below)*

Fairbourne & Barmouth Railway *(above)*
Kirklees Light Railway *(below)*

Lappa Valley Steam Railway *(above)*
Launceston Steam Railway *(below)*

Snowdon Mountain Railway
(above)

South Tynedale Railway *(left)*

Welsh Highland Railway
(Porthmadog) *(left)*

Welshpool & Llanfair Light Railway
(below)

West Lancashire Light Railway
(right)

West Somerset Railway
(below)